QUIET RAGE

QUIET
R·A·G·E

Bernie Goetz
in a Time of Madness

Lillian B. Rubin

FARRAR, STRAUS & GIROUX

NEW YORK

3-15-95

Library of Congress Cataloging-in-Publication Data
Rubin, Lillian B.
Quiet rage.
1. Goetz, Bernhard Hugo.   2. Victims
of crimes—New York (City)—Biography. I. Title.
HV6250.3.U53N4857 1986   364.1'552'0924 [B] 86-1843

For Roger

QUIET RAGE

1. Gathering speed as it moves out of the Fourteenth Street station, the train soon is hurtling through the dark tunnel that threads its way beneath the streets of New York City. Inside a grimy, graffiti-covered subway car some twenty women and men sit, close yet separated from one another, shielded from contact not just by the padding of their heavy winter clothing but by the psychological barriers they long ago learned to erect as they seek a few feet of space they can call their own, at least for as long as they occupy it.

Some are reading—a book, a magazine, a newspaper; one man dozes. Two women, friends who have been out shopping, are talking animatedly, reliving the day's activities, sharing plans for the Christmas holiday just three days ahead. A husband and wife sit wrapped in sullen silence, the aftermath of a quarrel. The rest just sit, eyes fixed and unseeing, bodies swaying and rolling to the rhythm of the train as it hurries on its way to the next stop.

A short, sharp sound rises above the familiar subway noises, and another. Heads come up, eyes become alert, glances meet inquiringly. For the first time, people actually see each other. My God, could it be? Gunshots? In the subway? Terror brings them together as they look about wildly, mutely seeking reassurance that their ears have deceived them. Then in quick succession, three more shots. There, down there at the other end of the car. Are people really lying bleeding on the floor?

The man with the gun turns toward them, a glint of light reflected from the chrome-plated weapon still in his hand. The nightmare of every New Yorker who rides the subway is about to be realized. Trapped! Trapped in this hideous, filthy, paint-smeared steel box. No place to run; nowhere to hide. Some people drop to the floor; others strain to open the heavy doors separating the cars as they seek safety in the next one. The rest cower—hoping, praying, the next blow won't fall on them.

With the train still moving at top speed, the conductor pulls the emergency brake. Steel meets steel with a sickening jolt, the string of cars lurching crazily before it finally screeches to a halt about a hundred yards short of the next station. For a few brief moments, train and people are still, set in a frozen tableau.

Only the gunman dares to move. Slight, blond, peering anxiously through his glasses, he walks among his fellow passengers, assuring them that the shooting is over. He leans over a woman lying on the seat and inquires politely if she's been hurt. Terror clutching her throat, she mumbles that she's fine. Bending down over a second woman, this one on the floor, he asks if she's all right. She's so frightened, she wants him to think she's dead. So she doesn't answer. He asks again. Unable to muster words, she shakes her head mutely.

The conductor, who can hardly believe anything else, thinks the shooter must be a police officer. Approaching cautiously, he asks, "Are you a cop?"

"No," the gunman mumbles, seeming somewhat dazed. "I don't know why I did it." Then: "They tried to rip me off."

With that, he walks to the doorway at the end of the car, open now because some passengers have fled through it, steps into the next car and, as people there watch fearfully, turns and jumps down onto the tracks and disappears into the yawning black tunnel.

2. By Sunday, December 23, New York City police have established a "Vigilante Task Force," and the manhunt is on for the subway gunman. As witnesses are interrogated, a description emerges from which the police artist can begin his work.

No one really knows what happened yet, only that a white man whose identity is unknown shot four black youths on a Manhattan subway. The victims of the shooting are Barry Allen, Darrell Cabey, Troy Canty and James Ramseur, eighteen and nineteen years old, all longtime residents of Claremont Village, a housing project in the South Bronx.

Most of the riders in the subway car saw nothing, knew nothing, until after the shots were fired. Among those who noticed the four blacks at the other end of the car before that, there's disagreement. Some say that they were just "horsing around," others that they were "acting rowdy."

Christmas Eve day. The city's tabloids headline the story, promptly dubbing the unknown assailant the "subway vigilante" and the "death wish shooter." The idea that a vigilante is on the loose, that a real live "death wish" killer is abroad, tantalizes both public and media. People read the stories avidly, turn on the television news eagerly.

The first police reports are out. The young men who were shot, they say, were carrying sharpened screwdrivers, dangerous weapons capable of killing. All four have arrest records. Allen, Canty and Ramseur have been convicted of misdemeanors ranging from disorderly conduct to criminal mischief and petty larceny. Canty and Allen each have a prior felony arrest as well—Canty for possession of stolen property, Allen for attempted assault. Only Cabey has no prior record, although he is under indictment for armed robbery, a felony to which he has pleaded not guilty.

The shooter, about mid-thirties—slight, blond, wearing wire-rimmed glasses—used a silver-colored .38 caliber pistol, make unknown. Ballistics reveals that two of the four bullets recovered were hollow-points, known in the gun world as dumdums—bullets which have been outlawed because they are designed to expand on contact and inflict maximum damage as they penetrate the flesh.

All the victims were hit in the upper body. Troy Canty was shot first, the bullet plowing through the center of his body, narrowly missing his heart. Barry Allen, who had turned to flee, got it next—in the back at the base of his neck. Then it was James Ramseur's turn to take the searing pain of one of the hollow-point bullets as it coursed through his arm and into his chest, destroying his spleen along the way. These three will walk out of the hospital one day, their bodies mended even though other scars will remain. The last victim, Darrell Cabey, was also hit with a dumdum bullet, this one fired at very close range—a missile that smashed its way through his body, tearing at flesh, bone and ligament as it pierced both lungs and severed his spinal cord. He will never walk again.

When they're able to talk with police, the boys say they don't know why the shooter pulled a gun and fired at them. They admit they were "foolin' around on the train when this white dude came in and sat down next to us." But they insist they did nothing to warrant his response. Yes, they all agree, Troy Canty did talk to him, but no one did anything to threaten him; no one had anything to threaten him with. Sure, the screwdrivers the police found in their pockets were theirs, but the gunman never saw them because they never took them out. They weren't sharpened either, as the press has been reporting; they were ordinary screwdrivers, useful for breaking into video-game machines.

As they tell it, Troy, who was sitting directly opposite the gunman, leaned over and said, "Hey, man, you got five dollars for me and my friends to play video games?"

"Yeah, sure," replied the man as he stood up. "I've got five dollars for each of you."

Before anybody could move, he whipped out a revolver and started to shoot.

The media hasten to bring the news to the public. Excitement is high. No one has yet heard the gunman's side of the story, only the words "They tried to rip me off." No matter. It's assumed by both press and public that a mugging has been thwarted, that some hoodlums carrying sharpened screwdrivers accosted a law-abiding citizen who turned the tables on them. This time it was the muggers who were left bleeding on the floor.

The public is mesmerized by this startling turn of events. Imagine! A man who resisted the muggers and got away with it. Nothing else matters; nothing else is noticed—not dumdum bullets, not that two people were shot in the back, not even that one is paralyzed for life. The newspapers and television broadcasts don't focus much on these facts; hardly anyone wants to hear them. "I don't give a damn where he shot 'em or how he did it," growls a man who regularly rides the subway into the city from Queens. "Those lousy punks deserve to die. God bless that man. When he pulled that gun, he was shooting for all of us."

The hot line established by the police is inundated with calls, not with the tips they hope will help them identify the gunman but with messages of support for him. Along the East River Drive, someone scrawls a message on the wall: POWER TO THE VIGILANTE; N.Y. LOVES YA! As they pass the crudely lettered words, drivers raise their fists in a victory salute and blow their horns to signal their agreement.

The police release an artist's rendering of the shooter, posting it in precincts, subway stations and other strategic spots around the city. Television stations and the press run the sketch, as police fan out in the neighborhood of Fourteenth Street, where the gunman is known to have boarded the subway, looking for something, anything, that will help them to identify this man. The New York *Post*, always seeking drama as it tries to get the jump on the competition, publishes the sketch on its front page under the headline "Subway 'Vigilante' " and appeals to him to turn himself in to its sympathetic city room.

Lost in all the noise is the corrected police statement—a statement that's at least partly due to the insistent probing and prodding of *Daily News* columnist Jimmy Breslin: The screwdrivers weren't sharpened after all; they were ordinary screwdrivers, just as the youths had been saying. And only two of the four were carrying these.

No one knows how the mistake was made; no one is held accountable. Certainly people, even cops, get excited in the middle of an investigation and things get said. But no one asks, either, why this particular thing was said. Yes, these young men have arrest records that would help to conjure such images and stimulate such fears. But the police who gave out the story on the scene and immediately afterward didn't know that then. All they had before them at the time were four black teenagers, each with a bullet in his body, and two with screwdrivers in their pockets.

Even the New York *Times* reporters, usually so careful in presenting the facts, miss this one. Days after the corrected statement is released, they're still writing about the sharpened screwdrivers. And a full week later, Phil Donahue, in a nationally televised program dealing with the shootings, suggests that the gunman was provoked by a quite comprehensible fear of the sharpened screwdrivers.

By the time the Christmas holiday is over, the city has gone wild. New York City has found itself a hero—a thin, blond, neatly dressed young man who, it seems, stood up and fought back against the punks who have turned its streets and subways into a nightmare of fear. At last! The facts, whatever they may be, are less important than the mood of triumph all around.

From all corners of the city come the hurrahs. Radio talk shows report hundreds of callers, almost all of them in favor of the attacker. On one show, a retired policeman calls to suggest, tentatively, that maybe the shooting wasn't necessary. When he was accosted by some young toughs, he says, he pulled his old service revolver and, at the sight of it, they ran. The host, WABC's Bob Grant, has already publicly mourned the fact that the shooter didn't do the job right and kill his victims. This time, he thanks the caller, then, just as he's about to hang up, adds, "Next time that happens, use the gun."

There are suggestions that the gunman be appointed police commissioner, elected mayor or governor, given the Congressional Medal of Honor, a place in the Hall of Fame. In a West Side subway station, someone draws a halo over his likeness. A noted New York criminal lawyer offers to represent him, saying, "He has expressed a blow for freedom—freedom from assault, freedom from rape, freedom from fear."

Television and newspaper interviews on the streets of the city show blacks as well as whites heavily in support of the shootings—responses the media keep reporting to confirm the view that race is not a factor in this public response. Roy Innis, head of the Congress of Racial Equality, calls the still unknown shooter "the avenger for all of us," adding, "Some black man ought to have done it long before. . . . I wish it had been me."

No black leader stands up to argue with him publicly, although many squirm privately. They're caught. They, too, are fed up with the young hoodlums who prey much more heavily on their own black community than on the white one. They, too, believe these kids deserve whatever they get. But for most of them, there's also the nagging question: Did the mystery gunman shoot *because* the youths were black? Is that at least partly what the celebration is all about?

As expressions of approval continue to pour in, political leaders become concerned. Two days after the shootings, Mayor Edward Koch calls the gunman's action "animal behavior" and promises an all-out effort to apprehend him. "A vigilante is not a hero," he cautions. . . . "You are not going to have instant justice meted out by anybody, because that's not justice. . . . It's wrong." In a caustic response to the mayor's statement, the Washington *Post* editorializes: "Mayor Koch has promised an all-out effort to solve the case, but the joke on the streets is that he just wants to find the gunman before the Republicans nominate him for mayor."

Police Commissioner Benjamin Ward warns against lionizing the gunman and pleads for restraint on the part of the media. But this is not *just* a media circus, not simply an event created by the excesses of press, radio and television.

It's certainly true that the media have helped to fan the flames that keep public passions burning so brightly. Day after day, the story makes the headlines, even when there isn't much to tell. Television news broadcasters stand on subway platforms as trains rush by, shouting into their microphones so as to be heard over the noise: "In a subway car just like this, the death wish killer unloosed the shots that will be heard for a long time to come." "Here, right on this station platform, the subway vigilante climbed up from the tracks and walked out into the street." In the race for news, reporters, whether print or broadcast, grasp avariciously at any bit of information, speculating here, embellishing there, some even making it up when all else fails.

In this way, the people who report the news have undoubtedly nourished the mood abroad. But they haven't manufactured the feelings now tumbling to the surface—the vengeful rage at the four young blacks who were shot, the exhilaration born of the belief that retribution has finally been exacted, the love affair with the unknown gunman. All this they are reporting quite accurately, if also flamboyantly. Calloused, cynical New York has fallen in love. Only nobody knows who the beloved is.

As the excitement continues unabated, a worried governor has some sharp words for the people of his state. "Throughout history, we've seen people whipped up by the sheer inability of the system to work for them," says Mario Cuomo. "People have supported the killing of millions of Jews, the imprisoning of the Japanese—and they thought they were right at the moment when their passion was turned up too high."

But by now, there's not much chance of turning the passion down. Instead, in just a few days, the case has become a national *cause célèbre*, making headlines in every corner of the land. "This is far more than a New York story; it's a story of human nature," says Geoffrey Alpert, the director of the University of Miami's Center for the Study of Law and Society. "It's something we'd all like to do. We'd all like to think we'd react the way he did."

3. The police are hard at work on the case even though, as some cops tell it, the response inside the force is much like the response outside. A small minority worries, reports an informant: "Some of the more thoughtful guys feel he went beyond the boundaries of what he had to do to defend himself. They feel he used more force than the situation warranted. Even if he was in danger, one shot would have sufficed."

Generally, however, policemen, just like the rest of the people of New York, read the situation quite differently. Although most have never met the youths who were shot, have only seen their pictures in the papers, they already know they don't like them. The word around the station house is that they're "arrogant and intimidating"; "the kind to bring out the bias in you—sassy, nasty"; "hoods who deserve what they got."

But for the cops there's also a certain ambivalence. They don't like the idea of ordinary citizens carrying guns. That's their turf and they don't want trespassers. As one detective puts it, "It's a problem; a gun's a dangerous weapon. You can't have people running around with a gun out there." Such reservations notwithstanding, however, he, along with several of his colleagues, also talks about sending money for the defense of the subway gunman. "Plenty of the guys are saying that after they catch him they'll contribute something to help the guy out."

As the days pass, the pressure inside the department is turned up. Word comes down from on high: Find the shooter. Manhattan's chief of detectives keeps a close watch on the investigation, visiting the detective unit assigned to the case almost daily. When he doesn't come in person, one of his deputies is there. Every day someone from upstairs is in the precinct, asking questions, making suggestions. Tension builds for the detectives on the case. With the brass breathing down their necks, they urge each other on: "Let's go; let's break this one."

They go back over every clue, talk once again to everyone involved. Some of the people on the train are good witnesses. But they have nothing to add. By now, three of the youths who were shot are feeling better, although still in the hospital. So they try again. They, too, don't have anything more to tell.

It's only a few days since the shootings, but it seems longer. So much din all around, so many words written, so many spoken, so much pressure to solve the case and nothing to go on. Finally they get the break they've been waiting for—an anonymous phone call.

The informant tells the police that he recognizes the man in their sketch. He saw him loading a silver-colored gun like the one that has been described and some of the bullets were copper-jacketed. If it's the same person, the man tells them, he was mugged once and swore that if anyone ever came at him again he'd "get the bastards."

His name: Bernhard Goetz. His address: 55 West Fourteenth Street. A name that would soon be known around the world. But for now, the police keep it quiet. It's just another lead.

Since guns require a permit in New York, the first task is to check the permit applications. Luck is with them. In 1981, Bernhard Hugo Goetz applied for a permit to carry a gun, saying it was necessary because he routinely carried large sums of money and valuables. The permit was denied: insufficient need. But all such applications require a photograph. Now the police have something with which to make a positive identification.

They take the photograph to the apartment building where Goetz lives and show it to the doorman. "Recognize this man?" He does. "Where can we find him?" They can't; he's gone away for a few days, the doorman tells them. They leave a note in Goetz's mailbox asking that he contact them as soon as he returns, go up to his apartment and slip a similar message under his door, and go back to the station house.

Satisfied that this is a good likeness of the man they're looking for, they have the photograph blown up and put into a photo array. This equivalent of a lineup, but with pictures instead of people, is made up of photographs of others who have the same general characteristics as Goetz. The detectives go back to their witnesses, show them what they have, and ask if they can identify the subway gunman. But their luck seems to have run out. Recalling the discouragement of the moment, one officer close to the case reports, "Unfortunately, our two best witnesses couldn't pick him out of the array. We knew the photo of him was a good one, but the witnesses were unsure, and when we pushed them, they said if they had to pick someone, they'd pick another guy."

Disappointed, and now uncertain that this is their man, the police try to turn their attention elsewhere. But they have little else to go on. This was their best lead, their only solid one. The detectives on the case are working long hours, no days off. They know they have to do something, but what?

They go back to Goetz's Fourteenth Street apartment, where the doorman tells them he has come and gone. "Did you tell Mr. Goetz we were looking to talk to him?" they ask. Yes, the doorman assures them, he did. Goetz went up to his apartment for a little while, he continues, then came down, said he'd be out of town again, and left. Helplessly, the police leave another note, this one tacked on his door, go back again to the precinct, and fiddle and fidget. They go over it all yet again; they follow up other clues they already know are useless. And they wait.

As the tide of public sentiment continues to swell, a few voices of opposition are raised, softly at first, barely heard over the roar of approval. Questions are asked: Don't people know that two of the youths were shot in the back? Or don't they care? Almost alone in the press, *Daily News* columnist Jimmy Breslin speaks out passionately against the glorification of the vigilante spirit that has overtaken the city. "We in New York have arrived at that sourest of all moments, when people become what they hate." He reminds his readers yet again that there were never any sharpened screwdrivers and that, as far as anyone knows, no screwdrivers of any kind were ever shown to the gunman.

Referring to the wounds sustained by Darrell Cabey, Breslin charges, "The bottom line is that people are rejoicing over a 19-year-old kid who will be in a wheelchair for a lifetime. I'm sorry, include me out." While on the other side, conservative columnist Patrick Buchanan, since named President Reagan's press chief, insists, "Far from being a manifestation of 'insanity' or 'madness,' the universal rejoicing in New York over the gunman's success is a sign of moral health. . . . Surely, among all the wounds inflicted on that subway system in calendar year 1984, Darrell Cabey's was almost the least undeserved."

December 31, nine days since the shooting, and still the police wait. But not for long.

Just after noon, at 12:10 to be exact, Bernhard Hugo Goetz, wearing the leather bombardier jacket that will soon become his trademark, walks into police headquarters in Concord, New Hampshire, and announces to the officer on duty that he's the person the New York police are looking for.

4. Inside the police station in Concord, the Watch Commander, Lieutenant Robert Libby, greets Bernhard Goetz. "He was very nervous," the officer says later, "extremely reluctant to speak with anyone around." Hoping to make the conversation easier, Libby clears the room. But it doesn't really help. "He rambled on, very nervous, shaking somewhat at times . . . afraid of what was going to happen to him back in NYC. . . . He also kept stating that the press were going to wipe the floor up with him, that he had violated so many laws, that they had no choice."

A puzzling concern. It hardly seems possible that the subway gunman had not read a newspaper, not heard a radio or watched a television news broadcast during his nine days of flight. Yet, if he had, why was he so fearful of the press, which, by then, had expressed its sympathies in its headlines?

When he finally calms down a little, Goetz is taken to an interrogation room by Officer Warren Foote, while the lieutenant goes off to advise the New York police that their suspect is in custody.

In New York, most of the members of the Vigilante Task Force aren't yet back from lunch when the phone rings at about

12:45. Inspector Rourke takes Lieutenant Libby's call and gets the news that Bernhard Goetz is being held in Concord, New Hampshire. In his report the lieutenant notes without comment that when they discussed the case, Rourke "stated that Goetz was a NY businessman, a basically good guy, sort of an electronics wizard." Some weeks later, however, Libby shakes his head in bemusement and with a wry smile says, "They must do things differently in the big city. It didn't sound to me like they were taking the whole thing very seriously down there. This guy was wanted for attempted murder, and he's telling me what a nice guy he is."

While the New York police move into action, Bernie Goetz spends the rest of the afternoon telling his story in Concord. At first, Officer Foote is alone with him, listening, asking questions, clarifying inconsistencies. "Can you describe the clothes you were wearing on the day of the shooting?" the officer asks. No problem. He was wearing a light blue jacket, blue jeans, a green plaid shirt and brown shoes—a description that matches exactly the information witnesses have already given to the New York police. Some of the clothes are still in his apartment, he says, but he burned the jacket somewhere in Vermont.

"What about the gun?" Foote wants to know. That, too, is in the woods in Vermont. "I broke it into pieces . . . actually smashed it," he says, and buried it in the snow somewhere north of Bennington.

"What kind of gun was it?" A .38 caliber Smith & Wesson, lightweight, nickel-plated, five-shot revolver. Two of the shells were standard load, the first two fired; the next three were hollow-points. "Let me explain," Goetz goes on to say, as he seeks to justify the unlawful dumdum bullets in his gun. "What you have to do, and I know this is gonna sound so criminal, you need the maximum stopping power, so you use something which is highly illegal." The newspapers, he complains, keep saying only four shots were fired. But they're wrong; he fired all five.

So he *has* read and heard the accounts of the shootings, the speculations about it and him. He must know, then, that he has captured the public imagination, that he has become the idol of media and public alike. His fear that the press would "wipe the floor up" with him becomes more baffling than ever.

"What happened after the shooting?" After he jumped off the train, he tells Foote, he ran south toward the Chambers Street station which, he guessed correctly, wasn't far away. When he got there, the end of the platform was deserted. He climbed up, went quickly to the steps and ran up to the street. There he slowed to a walk so he wouldn't attract attention, hailed a cab, got out at Fifteenth Street and walked to his apartment on Fourteenth Street. Once inside, however, he knew he couldn't stay there. So he showered hurriedly, started to disassemble the gun, changed his mind, packed a few things in a small suitcase, and left the apartment, telling the doorman he'd be away for a few days.

By three o'clock, little more than an hour after the shootings, he had rented a car and was on his way to Bennington, Vermont, where he registered in a motel under a false name. He doesn't know the name of the motel and can't remember what name he used, perhaps Fred Adams, someone he'd done work for in the past.

The flat, no-affect prose that characterizes police reports gives no sense of what Bernhard Goetz was feeling during those first hours of flight. Yet surely he must have been afraid—afraid of being caught, of being imprisoned, of being marked in some yet unknown way by what he had done. It's impossible to read the report without wondering: How does a man feel when he has just shot four people—a man who, until the moment he pulled the trigger, had lived mostly by the rules? What must he experience, this man who has stood always on the sidelines of life, when he finds himself the most sought-after person in the nation?

As the interrogation continues, Goetz talks about his days of wandering about New England, barren now in midwinter, scattered patches of snow the only reminders of the storm that fell before an unseasonal late-December thaw. He moved about restlessly during most of his nine days as a fugitive, went from Vermont to New Hampshire, from one town to another, usually registering under assumed names and giving false addresses.

He came to New England, he says, because he likes it. Unlike New Yorkers, the people are friendly and nice; it's clean and, most of all, safe. He grew up in the country, on a farm, he tells the police; that's where he learned to shoot a gun. And this area of New Hampshire reminds him of his hometown. Yet there's a vagueness about his account, things he can't remember or won't tell. No one knows for sure.

When police trace his movements afterward, they can account for some of his days but not all of them. They know he checked into the Mount Sunapee Motel in New Hampshire on Christmas Eve and spent the next two days and nights there. "He was just a regular customer who was very nice and polite," says the owner, Barbara Beliveau, when questioned.

After he left the motel, he wandered about the Sunapee–Sutton area aimlessly, staying a night here, a night there. One afternoon, as he was driving along a remote section of a highway about four miles outside the hamlet of Warner, he came upon a small, hand-painted sign which read "Old Paper World." The arrow on the sign pointed to an old wooden cabin set back about a hundred feet from the road. Apparently curious, he swung his car into the small clearing in front of the building, parked, and went inside. There he found himself in a shop crammed with thousands of old books, photographs, prints and other paper collectibles.

Tom Stotler, a short, heavyset man in his late sixties, who owns the store, is prominent in one of New Hampshire's several right-wing groups. Talking about the people who belong to these groups, one of the locals quips, "Some of those guys are about a quart low, as we say up here." Another describes them in a more serious tone. "They're the kind of people who believe in the law of men, not the law of the land. They're big on guns and property rights and things like that. Our motto up here is 'Live Free or Die,' and these people interpret it very literally"—a description Stotler probably wouldn't disagree with.

Recalling that first meeting with Bernie Goetz some time later, Stotler, who became one of Bernie's most outspoken and ardent supporters, says, "I could see from his license plates that he was from New York. But at first he didn't say anything to me, so I didn't say anything to him either. He spent about twenty minutes looking through some books, then said, 'Boy, you got some great old science books.' Then he looked around for another twenty minutes or so, and eventually I started a conversation with him by saying, 'How's it going down in New York?' He looked startled and said, 'How'd you know I was from New York?' I laughed and told him not to get nervous, I saw the plates on his car.

"We bounced around that a bit, and finally he really opened up and talked about what it's like in New York and how much crime there is on the streets. He told me about how he was mugged and how the guy who did it got caught and was let go, and he, Bernie, was held at the police station for the whole damn day. Then he talked about how it cost him two thousand dollars to try to get a gun permit, and after all that, they refused to give it to him. He was very angry about that. And I think it's an outrage—a violation of the Second Amendment. I don't know why good Americans stand for it. Anyway, that's the way the conversation with him went, just general like that. So when he turned himself in, I was sure surprised.

"When I read they were holding him, my son Chris and I went down to Concord to give him a little moral support. And ever since then, we've been good friends. I talk to him every couple of weeks; I just call to find out what's happening and to wish him luck. There's only two or three people he always talks to when they call, and I'm one of them."

Goetz's movements get lost for a day or two after his meeting with Stotler. Then, on the afternoon of December 29, he telephoned Myra Friedman, a neighbor.

When she was awakened from a nap by the ringing of the telephone, Ms. Friedman says, she heard a voice saying familiarly, "Myra, this is Bernie." She scurried around in her mind trying to think who this might be, as she sought unsuccessfully to place the person attached to the voice. "I don't know any Bernie," she thought to herself. And aloud: "Bernie who?" "Bernie Goetz," came the reply.

For Myra Friedman, the telephone call and its aftermath had a surreal quality, as she would soon tell the world in an article in *New York* magazine. Surprised that this man she hardly knew would be calling her, Friedman writes, she started to ask, "Bernie, what in the world . . . ?"

He cut off her question. "Listen, can you rent a car?"

"Rent a car? What are you talking about?"

"Do you know where Route 95 is to Connecticut?"

"Connecticut! What are you talking about?"

"Please, just listen to me. You can get a map and figure it out. Route 95. Take Route 95 to Connecticut, go off at Exit 6, and meet me at the Howard Johnson's there with a couple of the Guardian Angels and a tape recorder."

Listening to this agitated voice speaking what she now calls his "provocative, enticing words" and his "cloak-and-dagger invitation," Ms. Friedman realized that this man who lived in her building, whom she saw in the elevator and the lobby, who was a member of their tenants' association, whose voice was now coming across the telephone wires from somewhere in Connecticut, was the subway gunman.

Friedman is a writer and journalist, the author of a biography of the late rock star Janis Joplin. In the days before Bernie's call came, she had been researching a story for which she was interviewing people over the telephone. Her tape recorder, therefore, was poised and ready. Now suddenly, without will or warning, she found herself thrust into the middle of one of the biggest stories of the decade.

She didn't meet him, of course. But, her mind awhirl with a thousand half-formed questions and thoughts, she pushed the button on her recorder without telling Bernie. The taping just happened, she now says, "a physical, reflexive, instinctive act in response to the astonishing event of the phone call." Whether instinct or a moment of decision, it was an act that, for good or ill, would thrust her into the middle of the uproar around the case of Bernhard Hugo Goetz.

The next morning, December 30, Bernie drove back to New York, turned in his rented car and returned to his apartment. That's when he found the notes the police had left for him. He knew then that he had been identified and was being sought. He knew, too, that it was risky to be there. But he needed the moment of peace that being in his own home brought.

As if to reassure himself that his life could still be normal, he spent the next hour or so attending to some of the mundane tasks of daily living—cleaning and ordering things in his apartment. He took a shower, changed his clothes, packed some clean things, gathered up some papers he wanted to take with him, and prepared to leave again. But first there was something else he had to do.

Once again he turned to Myra Friedman. He knocked on her door softly, slipping inside as soon as she opened it. Holding out a neatly folded paper sack, he asked, "Would you keep this for me for a couple of days?"

When she looked at the package doubtfully, he assured her, "This is not the weapon that was used."

He went toward her bedroom to find a hiding place, she reports, while she stood somewhat dumbfounded. Finally: "No, not there," she gasped, pointing instead to the front closet. "Will it explode?" she asked him worriedly.

"No," he assured her, "there are no bullets in there," as he stowed his cache of guns out of sight on the shelf.

Friedman, already in a dilemma over how to deal with the knowledge that Bernie Goetz was the subway gunman, now became even more perplexed. What could, should, she do about it? As a law-abiding citizen, one who hated guns and violence, she couldn't sit quietly with the information. As an empathic woman who had listened to Bernie's tense, disjointed words on the telephone, who had witnessed his agitation when he stood in her living room, she didn't want to be the one to hurt him worse than he had already hurt himself.

But even as she mulled the options before her, the ominous package in her front closet kept intruding into her consciousness. No matter what the cost, she knew she had to get rid of it. But how? An attorney friend who might help was away for the weekend. So she waited—anxiously, fretfully.

As for Bernie, his last task was now done; the guns, he believed, were safely hidden. He left the building, rented another car, and by two o'clock that afternoon was on his way back to New Hampshire. There he checked into the Ramada Inn in Keene, registered under his own name, but gave his family's Florida address, and tried to sleep.

Early the next morning, he called Ms. Friedman again. As in the first call, his talk was nervous, inconsistent and disconnected, seeming to swing between grieving and being aggrieved, between being pained about what had happened on the subway and a self-righteous defense of his actions. He knew by then that he had to turn himself in, that he couldn't run anymore. But he was frightened and worried about what would happen when he did. What would they do to him? Would they believe his story? Would they understand that he *had* to do it, that he had no choice? How could he explain that those guys on the train were torturing him when he couldn't say exactly what they were doing? He had to make the police understand, as he kept trying to make Friedman understand, that he knew what was in their minds, that those people didn't have to say or do anything, that you could tell by the look in their eyes. If you lived in New York, you knew; you just knew.

This time he was concerned, also, about the package in her closet. Friedman asked if she could get into his apartment to return it. No, he said, he had the only set of keys. Besides, he thought it would be damaging for him if the guns were found there. After offering several suggestions about what she might do with them—ask a friend to put them in a hatbox, deny she knew what was in the package when and if she was questioned, drop them in the river from the Staten Island ferry, all of which Friedman rejected—the subject was dropped.

In fact, as soon as the long New Year's weekend passed, Ms. Friedman took the package from her front closet and delivered it to a lawyer, who turned it over to the district attorney. Before many more days passed, she would be questioned by the DA, the tapes of her conversations with Bernie would be subpoenaed, and she would appear as a witness before the grand jury hearing the case.

QUIET RAGE

. . .

For the rest of the morning, Bernie Goetz drove around the
New Hampshire countryside, his head spinning with the anxious
questions he had earlier spoken to Myra Friedman. He had no
particular destination, just kept driving until, finally, the time had
come. Sometime around noon, he sought out the police station in
Concord, walked in and, so nervous he was barely coherent, gave
himself up.

5. The Bronx—the northernmost of New York's five boroughs, the Harlem River bounding its western shore, Long Island Sound on its eastern flank. Starting at its southern end, the Grand Concourse, a boulevard whose name is a reminder of earlier dreams of grandeur, divides east from west as it wends its way through the length of the borough.

Not so long ago the Bronx was a haven for the upwardly mobile immigrant families escaping from the crowded, noisy life of Manhattan's Lower East Side. There were some single-family and two-family dwellings there then, even as a few remain today, especially in the northern sectors. But for most people, life still was lived in apartment buildings, albeit buildings with a difference. Each apartment had its own bathroom. And the rats and roaches that were so much a part of life in the ancient tenements of Manhattan hadn't yet found their way so far north.

True, it was still crowded inside the apartment. Very often the living room served also as a bedroom, sometimes housing Uncle Tony or Aunt Frieda—the most recent arrivals from the old country—sometimes accommodating parents who gave over the only real bedroom to their children. Sometimes, too, a bed in the living room was the only means of separating brothers and sisters as they entered puberty and parents began to worry about their emerging sexuality.

But outside, the streets were quieter, not teeming with people and commerce. On some streets there were even a few trees. Some neighborhoods boasted a park—large ones like Van Cortlandt Park or Bronx Park with its zoo, where the whole family could enjoy a Sunday, and smaller ones, patches of green to bring respite from the concrete and steel all around, places where adults could meet and children could play.

Since it was closer to Manhattan, where most people worked, the southern half of the Bronx was more densely populated than its northern areas. The more affluent lived right on the Concourse in buildings that seemed grand then, built of a buff-colored brick instead of red. To the children who lived on streets darkened by the dingy red brick buildings that dominated most neighborhoods, these seemed bathed in light and sunshine.

From the Concourse west to the banks of the Harlem River the respectable, upwardly mobile working class and lower middle class shared the streets with families already settled into the middle class. And even all those years ago, the east side was largely the preserve of those who were less fortunate—the poor and the near-poor.

Whether east or west, however, for the people who went there then, the Bronx was a place of hope, often the first step on the road to the American dream. Not everyone who moved to the Bronx took the next step, of course. But even if they couldn't, they could believe their children would.

That's not true anymore. The Bronx no longer takes in the huddled masses from foreign shores. Now it's largely "real" Americans who people its streets and live in its houses. Black Americans for whom the hope faded, the dream went sour a long time ago.

Today, Claremont Village, a housing project whose immensity belies its name, is situated in the heart of the southeastern sector of the Bronx known as the Morrisania district. No one in New

York City's Housing Authority seems to know for sure how many apartments there are in the project, partly perhaps because some are still under construction or have only very recently been completed. Guesses range from 2,000 to 3,000 units. Even less is known about how many people live there. Some Housing Authority estimates say 7,500, others are as high as 10,000.

This vast expanse of barren red brick buildings—each twenty-one stories high, each exactly like the other—has the unmistakable mark of New York City's public housing projects. Cold, forbidding, meager—the project's silhouette dominates the landscape, its towering buildings thrusting skyward belligerently, ominously, their hard, sharp edges unrelieved by any architectural amenities.

Since they were built over a period of years, there are some small differences in the interiors of the buildings. But generally Claremont Village is no lovelier, no less bleak, no more human in scale on the inside than on the outside. In some, the lobby is hardly wider than a normal hallway and smaller than an ordinary room, the first clue to the stinginess with which these public housing projects are built. Enter these buildings and you feel your body constricting, shoulders hunching up, pulling in, as if by making yourself smaller you'll find some protection from the dingy gray walls that threaten to close in on you.

With hundreds of apartments in each building, these tiny lobbies are busy places. The elevators scurry up and down constantly as people come and go, their senses shut down so they need not notice its ugly stench. The corners, which often are no more than a couple of arm lengths away, may be the meeting places where dope deals are made or the resting places for the drunks and junkies of the neighborhood.

Some buildings have wider lobbies, their walls lined with garish yellow tiles instead of the toneless gray of the others. In these, members of the Tenants' Council, mostly women, may be seated at a table, asking everyone who enters to sign in, part of the community effort to control crime in the stairways, hallways and elevators.

Especially the elevators. Above the ground instead of under it, still the elevator carries the same menacing force as the subway car—a steel box from which there's no escape. "Don't ride the elevator by yourself when you come up to visit," warns the mother of one of the youths who was shot. "Y'never know what'll happen. Anybody's got to watch for trouble in the elevator, but a stranger, especially a white woman, you'd be a sure victim."

But the tenants' patrols are concerned with crimes against their own, not against some stranger who happens to wander in, not against the world outside. For it is the people in the neighborhood who are the most frequent targets of the young criminals in their midst, who are the most likely to fall prey to the petty crimes and the brutal ones, the crimes against property and those which assault persons, all of them part of everyday life in Claremont Village.

It is the people in the neighborhood, too, who pay the price for the abundance of drugs on the street, as all too often they stand by helplessly watching their children being seduced into the drug culture and from it into crime. Walk down the streets of Claremont Village and even the unaccustomed eye cannot miss the pushers plying their trade; the users sniffing, swallowing, injecting the stuff into bruised and battered veins. "Once the kids get out on these streets, they're lost," says Eula Canty, Troy's mother. "It's mostly the drug problem that turns most of the kids around. That's what it was with Troy, I know. Drugs is all over the streets—marijuana, cocaine, heroin. He wasn't into heroin, just marijuana and cocaine. But you know, they don't have no good stuff up here, so who knows what he was taking. It's mixed with Lord knows what."

The apartments themselves have the same cold, confined, unlovely feel as the buildings. In some, the tenants obviously have given up hope, and the inside of the apartment is no better than the outside. But many show the results of enormous efforts to create an environment that's different—walls covered with vinyl paper in the hope of containing the peeling paint, furnishings, even when old, tended with painstaking care and tastefully arranged. "When I started to work, I had three choices," recalls a Claremont Village woman. "To buy a car, or take a plane trip, or fix up the house. Well, I never got up the nerve to learn to drive, and I never got on no plane either. So there was nothing else but to try to fix up the house. I redid my living room, and now it looks very nice," she says, smiling proudly.

But no amount of fixing can stretch the tiny, cramped rooms, or widen the hallways, so narrow that your shoulders nearly brush the walls, or put closets and cupboards where there are none. No amount of fixing can keep these places warm in the winter or cool in the summer. No amount of fixing can make a two-bedroom apartment adequate to house six people, can stop the squabbling of kids who haven't even a small corner of space to call their own, can assuage the restlessness or satisfy the yearnings that dominate their young minds and bodies.

So the streets beckon, drawing the young people of the project to them like a magnet, seeming to promise a place to expand, to move, to breathe free. But once the kids are on them, the streets become their own kind of prison.

"Y'hardly never saw a white face 'round here 'til the shootings. Now the newspaper reporters and TV people are all over the place," mumbles a Claremont Village man angrily.

The shootings. No need to be more explicit. Mention "the shootings" and every New Yorker remembers that Saturday afternoon just before Christmas when radio and television flashed the news that a white man had shot four black youths on the

#2 IRT downtown express. For the people of Claremont Village, however, these were not just "four black youths." These were their children. When the news came that Barry Allen, Darrell Cabey, Troy Canty and James Ramseur were from the project, every parent there cringed as if falling away from a blow. For they knew with dread certainty that these boys might have had other names, that the kid with a hole in his body might have been theirs.

It's not that every young man in Claremont Village is troubled or in trouble. But the potential is there for all of them. "I tried so hard to make a home where the kids would like to stay in it," says Shirley Cabey, Darrell's mother. "I bought this stereo, a nice TV, just so's they could listen to their music here, y'know, so they'd stay home where I'd know what they're doing. But you can't keep them locked up, hard as you try. Lord knows, I tried. Then they get to a certain age, and what can you do? I'd tell all of them, there ain't nothing but trouble out there on those streets. All those kids just hanging there; no school, no jobs, nothing to do, no place to go. Just cooking up trouble."

Washington and Third—a tough corner in a tough neighborhood, one of the community training grounds for turning boys into men, hardened men, all too quickly. Here they swagger and posture, testing out their emerging manhood, showing off for one another, for the girls, for their younger brothers. Here they find companions in hopelessness, others like themselves with whom to share their rage.

They're just kids, but they don't look like kids. No sign of the vulnerability, of the searching, of the anxieties and the fears so common among teenagers. Can it be that there is no fear, just this cold, impenetrable hardness? Or is it there but hidden from view? Hidden behind eyes that long ago had already seen too much suffering, too much brutality, too much defeat. Where is the future in Claremont Village? "Ain't no use in going to no school; can't get no job worth shit anyways," mumbles Ralph, a sixteen-year-old habitué of the corner.

So they lay their plans, scheme their schemes. What do you want? Drugs? Booze? A scam to make a few bucks? A gun? A knife? Name it. If it's not here, they know where to find it. They know also that they might not be back on the corner tomorrow, that today's action could land them on Rikers Island, the prelude to another sixty-day stint in jail or the rehab center. So what? "Those motherfuckers can't scare me; I can take care of myself," boasts seventeen-year-old Lewis.

Every once in a while someone disappears from the corner for good, sent to an early grave by some violent encounter, sometimes with the police, more often with others like themselves, in prison or out. What difference does it make? Prison, death, the streets—it's all the same. "Might as well be dead as stand around waitin' for a fuckin' handout from the man," says Merrill tonelessly.

Barry Allen, Darrell Cabey, Troy Canty, James Ramseur—four of the dozens of Claremont Village kids whose psychological home is the corner of Washington and Third. Now they lie in hospital beds, slowly recovering consciousness, feeling for the spot from which pain flows. "Christ, it hurts like hell."

Most of their parents had heard about the shootings from news reports that had been broadcast since midafternoon. But it never occurred to any of them to think their sons were involved. It's a long way from the Bronx to lower Manhattan, a trip these parents seldom, if ever, made. The ninety-cent subway fare was enough to discourage frivolous travel even if they wanted to go there. So there was no reason to think this had anything to do with them.

Now, in separate hospital rooms—two in Bellevue, two in St. Vincent's—members of the families sit stiffly in hard chairs, thinking their own thoughts, feeling their own pain. They all knew that they had long ago lost control of this son who was now lying so still in his bed, that the model of their own difficult and impoverished lives was no match for the lure of the streets. But like all parents who must confront the fact that they are ineffective in controlling their growing children's behavior, they managed to deny the reality before their eyes.

Different behaviors will generate such parental denial, the differences depending on the values associated with class, race and culture. But all parents will manage not to know what they know when knowing is too painful. Indeed, this kind of denial is a common human response in any situation where we feel helpless to effect change, whether about something so large as a nuclear holocaust or about the despised behavior of a teenage or adult child.

The parents of Barry Allen, Darrell Cabey, Troy Canty and James Ramseur worried about their sons, but they denied what they knew and continued to hope that their child's fall was only temporary, that this young man who sometimes seemed like such a stranger would magically become again the boy they once knew. "Troy was always such a quiet boy, never gave me no trouble. So I figured things would straighten out for him, that, you know, he'd be all right. Maybe now, after all this, it'll be different," says Eula Canty hopefully. Asked what she thinks will happen to make the difference, her eyes seek the window which looks out on the street as she shrugs helplessly: "I don't know. I guess I got to keep hoping, but those streets out there; I just don't know."

In one of the rooms, the boy on the bed begins to move about restlessly. The anesthetic hasn't yet finished its work, so it's hard to focus, hard to remember where he is, how he got there. The frightened faces of loved ones swim into view as the visitors gather around anxiously, murmuring quiet, soothing words, touching him gently. "Mama, I'm sorry." "What happened, son?" "I don't know, mama; it all went down so quick; hard to remember."

He's scared now. He wants to reach out, to let her hold him like she used to, just this once. But his arms might as well be made of lead. Tears well up, bringing an unaccustomed stinging behind his eyes. But even now he won't let them fall. Instead, his lids flutter downward, covering the bright shimmering that might give him away. "I'm tired, mama; need to sleep."

For this mother as for all the others, there is no sleep on this night—just haunting, painful questions. And the prayer: Please, God, let him be all right.

6· As he listens to Bernie Goetz's rambling, sometimes in-coherent tale, Officer Foote's attention begins to wander. He shifts his body around, trying to find a position in which he won't be so distracted. He doesn't want to stop the flow of words, only the irrelevant ones.

So while Goetz talks angrily about the time he was mugged back in 1981, about the inhumanity of the New York City police, about their incompetence, Foote wonders how to get him back to the story he's after. He wants him to talk about what went on in the subway, about why he shot those four young men. Finally, he asks.

Goetz responds with more talk about the dangers of living in New York City, about the inability of the police to protect innocent people. "Several times during this interview, Mr. Goetz stated that he did not feel that what he had done was wrong," Foote writes in his report. "He stated that what he did was cold-blooded, but the system would not take care of it, this is the reason why he had to carry a firearm while he walked around New York City."

Foote asks what prompted him to use the gun. Goetz describes the scene on the subway, where the boys were sitting when he entered, where other passengers in the car were seated. "Mr.

Goetz stated when he entered the car, he noted two negro males sitting on either side of the door he entered; he also noted two negro males across from the door, sitting on the bench. He noted other people in the car, but they were at the front of the car."

He tells how, with about twenty passengers seated at one end of the car, he took a seat at the other end, right next to the black youths he would soon shoot. He offers to draw a diagram showing where they all sat, an offer Foote accepts gratefully.

After he sat down, one of the young men asked him how he was doing. He answered, saying he was fine. "Mr. Goetz stated that he thought this was funny, also stated that at this time he did not feel that was a threat."

A short time after the train left the station, he says, two of the boys got up and walked over to his left. One of them, the youth who had spoken to him originally, spoke again, this time asking him for five dollars. "Mr. Goetz stated that this in itself was not a threat. He looked at the gentleman's face and noted he was smiling and his eyes were shining. . . . Mr. Goetz stated he stood up and in doing so he noted . . . one of the negro males to his right put his hand in his pocket and made like he had a weapon of some type there. Mr. Goetz went on to state that . . . he did not feel threatened by this move." Quite the contrary. "That was bullshit," Bernie told Foote. "I knew that they didn't have a gun there. These guys aren't that stupid; that's just part of the game." In fact, he explained that by then he already knew he would use his gun: "I'd already laid down my pattern of fire."

Events moved quickly once his decision was made. Seconds after he got to his feet, Bernie Goetz pulled his pistol from its fast-draw holster, leaned against a post to steady himself and, holding the gun in firing position with both his hands, fired four shots as he methodically and efficiently executed his plan of attack.

"He stated that after firing the four shots, he went back to check the first two subjects who were now lying on the floor of the subway car. After checking them . . . he went to the second two subjects, one being on the floor, the other . . . half sitting, half lying on a bench where he was originally. Mr. Goetz stated then that he saw no blood on the subject. At that time . . . he shot the fourth subject a second time."

Concluding his report, Foote says of Bernie Goetz, "He did not feel threatened by the subject asking him how he was, or asking him for five dollars; it was the whole total situation that caused the shooting. Mr. Goetz stated that he thought it was funny that these four black subjects thought they had him trapped, when in fact they were trapped." In Bernie's own words, Canty and Allen "tried to run through the crowd and, of course, they had nowhere to run because the crowd would stop them. And I got them. . . . The other guy," referring to Ramseur, "tried to run through the wall of the train, but . . . he had nowhere to go."

After about an hour and a half of interrogation, Foote and Goetz are joined by Detective Christopher Domian. The two policemen confer briefly; they decide to take a taped statement in addition to the one he has already given. Another two hours of interrogation ensue. Throughout, Goetz is cooperative, even talkative, words spilling out rapidly, albeit incoherently at times, although Foote reports, "When giving the taped statement, Mr. Goetz seemed to be a lot more calm than he was when I originally talked to him."

In a separate report, Detective Domian confirms Foote's account almost down to the last detail. Commenting on Goetz's decision to shoot, he writes: "He indicated that they showed no outward signs of being armed or a danger to him . . . and went on to say that he felt just the body language of the individuals was enough to tell him what was going to be done at that particular time. He indicated he has been a long enough resident of New York to know the body language of the individuals and what their intentions were."

Goetz complained, Domian says, that they "were playing with him like a cat and a mouse" and that long before a shot was fired, he had already drawn "a pattern of fire . . . indicating that he was going to shoot from left to right in the quickest and most effective manner possible. He indicated speed was everything."

"Your intention was to shoot these people?" asked Domian.

"My intention was to do anything I could do to hurt them. . . . My intention was to murder them, to hurt them, to make them suffer as much as possible."

Both Foote and Domian note that Bernie Goetz never gave the slightest indication that he felt any remorse about the shootings. "If I had had more bullets, I would have shot them again and again and again."

By midafternoon the interrogation by the local police is over. But for Bernhard Goetz, there's no respite. At about six o'clock, Manhattan Assistant District Attorney Susan Braver arrives, followed a half hour later by Detectives Dan Hattendorf of the New York Transit Police and Michael Clark of the NYPD. The questioning begins anew.

Only this time the suspect is surly, uncommunicative and uncooperative. "As soon as Mr. Goetz was led into the library and introduced to the New York detectives, he immediately became hostile towards them," reads a police report. He doesn't want to answer their questions, doesn't want to be in the same room with them. He trusts the Concord police, he says, but not those from New York. Eventually, he agrees to talk, but only, he assures them, to give them enough information to convince them that he's the man they've been looking for in connection with the subway shootings.

His hatred of New York is palpable, a living thing inside him. For him, it's a dying city, a modern Sodom and Gomorrah, deserving of the same fate. He distrusts its criminal justice system, which, he insists, cares nothing for decent, law-abiding, honorable citizens. Only when these good people rise up against this monstrous situation will the city be saved. He can find not one good word for the city or its officials. "He went as far as to tell them that he didn't even like their New York accent," reports one amused observer.

He doesn't like Susan Braver either, tells her she knows nothing about New York and what goes on there on its streets and in its subways. The city has no right to send someone with so little knowledge to interview him, he complains. "Several times during the interview he became agitated with questions that were asked by the NY DA, and it appeared to me that he resented the fact that she was even in the room with him," notes the officer who ran the video equipment during this part of the interrogation.

Meanwhile, Captain Charles Prestia, Manhattan Commander of Detectives, informs Detective Domian that Bernhard Goetz will be charged with four counts of attempted murder and four counts of assault in the first degree. The Concord police call upon New Hampshire Assistant Attorney General Andrew Isaac to assist in the drawing of the complaint. At 12:45 in the morning Judge Vincent Dunn signs it and sets bail.

At 1:10 a.m., thirteen hours after he walked through the door of the Concord police headquarters, Bernhard Hugo Goetz is finally arrested and formally charged. New Year's Eve has come and gone. It's now early in the morning of the first day of the year. Finally, he can get some rest. But he takes with him the knowledge that his bail has been set at $500,000 cash.

7.
Back in New York, Goetz's neighbors are being roused
out of their New Year's Eve plans by reporters banging on their
doors with requests for interviews. As one neighbor tells it: "We
heard the news about Bernie at about four o'clock on New
Year's Eve. Some reporters from the *Daily News* rang the bell,
and I thought they were trying to sell a subscription. I couldn't
believe it when they told me he was the vigilante. We always
knew he was weird and kind of flaky, but *that*?"

Another, stunned at the impact the news has had on his life,
says: "It was New Year's Eve day, about four o'clock. I was
taking my dirty underwear down to the laundry, and just as I
got in the elevator, this guy jumps in and says, 'Do you live
here?' I thought: 'This guy must be crazy. What would I be
doing with my dirty laundry in the elevator if I didn't live
here?' Then he asks, 'Do you know Bernhard Goetz?' 'Sure,' I
said, 'he's my neighbor.' And then he drops this bombshell. 'Do
you know that he's the subway vigilante?'

"I just kind of stood there with my mouth open; I didn't
know what to say. I couldn't say what I was thinking because
I didn't want to get him in any more trouble than he was already
in, so I just said some things that were kind of neutral. But what

I really thought was: 'Of course, he's crazy; I always knew he was crazy, everybody does, and I always worried that he was kind of dangerous.' Like I said, he was always one strange dude, and he kept getting stranger and stranger.

"Within minutes," he continues, shaking his head in wonder as the memory returns, "a thunder of TV cameras arrived, and from then on, it was unbelievable. My phone never stopped ringing. I'd already told them everything I knew; I didn't have anything else to say, but they kept coming and coming."

As the afternoon wears on and the news spreads through the building, other neighbors, members of a community organization called "For A Better (FAB) 14th Street," in which Goetz is an active member, gather to talk about the startling events of the day. Some of those who come together on this last day of the year have been sympathetic with the subway vigilante from the start, and the discovery that he is a neighbor only increases their excitement. Others have always been ambivalent, an ambivalence that is not diminished when his identity becomes known. Despite these differences, however, all agree to see what, if anything, they can do to help this man they variously describe with words ranging from "sweet" and "shy" to "quirky" and "dangerous." So plans are laid for the establishment of a defense fund, and discussions held about how to find him an attorney.

One of the men in the group, himself an attorney, volunteers to speak to Bernie in the Merrimack County jail where he's being held. "We thought if we were going to get together a defense fund, we should know if he was willing to accept our help. When I finally got to him, he said he didn't want anything, no fund, nothing.

"He was very, very depressed and dejected, and said that whatever would happen to him would happen. Being a lawyer, naturally, I didn't like to hear something like that. Irrespective of what happened on the subway, I thought he was entitled to a defense. Also I was intrigued by the case and the substantial legal issues involved. I knew it would present some challenging and knotty problems."

While some journalists are working the New York beat, others are rushing up to New Hampshire to meet the man who is already becoming a legend. For the next three days, dozens of reporters congregate outside police headquarters, trailing after Goetz as he is taken from the station house to jail to court and back again, waiting for a word, a glimpse, a chance to take a picture—anything they can show or tell their hungry public.

By now, ten days after he shot four youths on a Manhattan subway, Bernie, as he has quickly become known, has become the symbolic embodiment of everyone's fantasies. He's the man who acts instead of talks, the guy who's mad as hell and isn't going to take it anymore. More important, he's done what others of us only dare think about.

"To tell you the truth, I wish'd I'd 'a done it myself," says a New York City cabdriver angrily. "Those goddamn kids have scared the whole city long enough, and Bernie showed them once and for all. We oughta give him a medal."

"Do you ever think about carrying a gun?"

"Jeez, lady, I thought about it, but . . . naw, I'd never pack a gun. I'm sure glad he did, though."

"Then you want someone else to do the dirty work? Is that it?"

Laughing at the question: "Maybe, you might put it that way. Thing is, I don't know if I could do it; that's why I don't carry no gun. If someone carries a gun, they gotta know they'll use it someday. Know what I mean? Naw, it's not for me."

It's not just the average guy on the street for whom Bernie Goetz has satisfied a longing. Others, more thoughtful, less at ease with the thoughts that come to them unbidden, nevertheless admit them. "I wish I could say I've never thought about it myself, but I can't," acknowledges a psychologist. "In fact, I can't tell you how often I've had the fantasy of getting one of those punk kids and working him over good, even killing him. Just thinking about it makes me feel better somehow, as if I've redeemed myself. That's why Goetz has struck such a chord. He did it; we get to savor it vicariously."

Even for those whose fantasies don't go this far, the case of the subway shootings has raised difficult and uncomfortable internal conflicts. Many people find themselves applauding an act that, in other circumstances, they know they would abhor. They don't like guns, don't approve of violence. Yet they can't contain the sense of pleasure, even gratitude, they feel in knowing that someone finally struck back.

Some people speak of being startled by the intensity of their own visceral reactions. "Until this whole thing happened, I didn't know I was so mad about what's happened to this society," muses a woman who lives in Greenwich Village and works as an attorney for one of the large corporations headquartered in Manhattan. "So I was really surprised at my reaction when I heard the news. My immediate response was: 'Good. Those damn kids deserve it.' It was only later, when I had some time to think about it, that I began to wonder about what really happened, and whether he really had to shoot all four of them, and things like that."

Others speak of feeling somewhat shamed by the force of the feelings that have been stirred within them. "I can't say I was proud of my reaction," says a man who twenty years ago participated in the drive to register black voters in the South. "Christ, I hate how I feel about these goddamn black kids, but they have everyone in this city living in terror. Yeah, yeah, I know this case isn't as clean as it could be. But there's no arguing yourself out of being glad anyway. That's what makes the damn situation so hard."

Even among people who know quite clearly that they don't

support Goetz, even among those who believed from the start that this was no clear-cut case of self-defense, there's a certain sympathetic understanding. "I don't like what he did, but . . ." they say. "I certainly don't approve of guns on the subway, but . . ." "I always thought it was overkill, but . . ." Always there's the "but," the doubt, the compassion, the connection of one human being with another that's born of shared experience. Who doesn't know what it's like to be afraid of kids like Allen, Cabey, Canty and Ramseur? And, if frightened enough, who knows for sure what any of us would do?

Not just in New York City but all around the country, such people are finding feelings and intellect at war in the case of the subway gunman. They remind themselves that they don't yet know the facts, caution themselves against getting caught up in the passions of the moment, talk to friends as they search for some way to resolve the conflict within them. But whether the friends share their conflicts or have joined the Goetz bandwagon without ambivalence, their conversations don't help much. So they continue to probe themselves and their motives, keep trying to bridge the gap between intellect and emotion, to make thoughts and feelings match. But it's hard when all around them the shouts of joy are so loud, especially so because the approving noise finds its resonance in their own hearts.

Like so many others, the media people, too, generally have a complicated set of responses. It's not just because it's a good story that they're so involved, not just because it's their job to report the news that they have come to New Hampshire so eagerly, that they tell the world what little they know with such relish. It's because they are one with us.

From the beginning, the newspaper reporters and television commentators, too, were captivated by the man they quickly dubbed the "subway vigilante." They, too, walk the streets and ride the subways in fear; they, too, are tired of "coddling the thugs"; they, too, live with fantasies of retribution; they, too, suffer ambivalence at the intensity of their own rage; they, too, wouldn't consider using a gun but relish the fact that somebody did.

Now, seeing this shy, self-effacing, clean-cut, blond Goetz, they're enchanted. Ironically, the only thing the subway gunman has to say to or about the reporters who hover over his every move during these days is: "Vultures!"

8 · Osnabrück, Germany. In this city located near the north-west corner of Germany, Bernie Goetz's father, Bernhard Sr., was born and raised, one of nine children brought up by a widowed mother. His father, George, had been killed in World War I.

Times were hard in Germany between the two world wars. The Great Depression had hit this vanquished nation earlier and harder than most, and jobs were scarce. Bernhard was among the lucky few to find work. But he was an ambitious young man, eager to make his mark in the world. And his job as a printer's apprentice held out little promise to satisfy his drive. So his eyes turned westward, toward America.

In 1928, at the age of twenty-two, he left his home town, his familiar life, his native land, and boarded a ship bound for the United States. Two weeks later, Bernhard arrived at Ellis Island, just another out of the hordes of penniless immigrants who sought their fortunes on these shores.

But he wouldn't stay that way for long. He quickly found a job with a bookbinding company that made sample books of fabric swatches and photograph albums to record ceremonial occasions such as weddings and bar mitzvahs. Tenacious and resourceful, a driven man whose ambition was the dominant force in his life, Bernhard Goetz seized every break that came his way—and undoubtedly created a few as well. A little more than a decade after his arrival in this country, he owned the company for which he had first gone to work.

Reflecting on the elder Goetz's early years in the United States, one man who knew him then says now, "I wasn't surprised to read in the papers he died a rich man. He was ambitious, that one—a worker, too. He never stopped. Anybody who knew Goetz knew he'd make it big one day. Seemed like it's what he lived for."

Not long after he began his climb upward, Bernhard met Gertrude Karlsberg, the woman who would become his wife. She, the daughter of a German-Jewish immigrant family, her father a successful importer; he, the German-Lutheran immigrant youth only recently arrived. Soon their lives would be joined together, the wedding held at the Tavern-on-the-Green, a chic and expensive restaurant in Manhattan's Central Park.

They were opposites, these two. By all accounts, she was a kind and gentle woman, passive and obedient to the will of her husband. She was a good listener; he could scarcely hear a voice that wasn't his own. He made money; she wrote poetry. He forswore religion; she embraced it. But not the Jewish religion of her own family. Instead, she converted to Lutheranism shortly after her marriage, raised her children as Lutherans, and remained a devout churchgoer for the rest of her life.

But on one thing they were agreed: the necessity to try to save at least some of the victims of Hitler's oppression. So as the news of religious and political persecutions began to filter out of his homeland, Bernhard became seriously involved in rescue efforts, sending money, offering guarantees of employment for the refugees he helped bring over.

. . .

Shortly after their marriage, Gertrude and Bernhard moved to an apartment in Elmhurst, in the borough of Queens. There their children were born: first the elder daughter, Barbara, then a son, George. After a gap of several years, two more children arrived: Bernice and finally the son who would be his father's namesake, Bernhard Hugo Goetz, born on November 7, 1947, at Kew Gardens Hospital and promptly nicknamed Boo Boo.

Over the years, the Goetzes discovered the Hudson River Valley, a hundred or so miles north of New York City. The whole area there was reminiscent of his native land: the lush green farmland, the clean fresh snow in winter, the cold wind coming off the river so like the icy breezes that sweep down on Osnabrück from the North Sea, the cool summers instead of the city's uncomfortable mugginess. Enchanted with the country-side, tired of the confines of city life, they bought a 200-acre dairy farm near the village of Clinton Corners in Dutchess County. For the next few years, the family's life was divided between New York and Clinton Corners. From Monday to Friday, they lived in the city, where Bernhard ran the company he owned by then, and weekends were spent tending the farm.

In 1949, when little Boo Boo was two years old, the family left Elmhurst entirely and moved to the farm. For the children, the move meant the freedom of wide, grassy pastures over which to roam and play. For Gertrude Goetz, the farm brought relief from the ever-present concern about the children's safety whenever they were out of the house. But whatever this bucolic life meant to the elder Bernhard, it couldn't engage him fully. So during this period, he not only ran the farm in Clinton Corners and maintained the factory in Manhattan, he also established the Silver Lake Dairy in Red Hook, another small town nearby. Very soon the dairy was distributing its products throughout eight neighboring counties.

Still his restless ambitions were unsatisfied, and he turned his attention to yet another new venture—this time, to real estate development. He bought a tract of land on the edge of a forest in nearby Rhinebeck where he eventually built three houses—one for the family, the others to be sold or rented. In a few years, the family moved from the farm to Rhinebeck. There they remained until 1963.

Rhinebeck, New York—a community founded in 1686 and settled by the Palatines, people from the land we now know as Germany. Lying just east of the Hudson River, it remains now as it must have been then, a lovely little village of rolling hills and vistas of not so distant mountains. It's easy to understand Rhinebeck's appeal to the German immigrants who settled there so eagerly, since both the climate and the geography of the area are reminders of the German Rhineland.

Even today, it's still not more than a fifteen-minute stroll to traverse every foot of Rhinebeck's half-mile-long commercial main street and the few side streets onto which shops have spilled to accommodate its growth. The present population of just over 7,000 is more than twice that of the early 1950s, when Bernie Goetz entered the lone elementary school there.

The Goetz house on Wynkoop Lane in Rhinebeck is part of a small cluster of modest homes belonging to people of modest means. A spare, unimaginative, uninviting structure located near the foot of the street—just above the juncture where Wynkoop Lane meets the main highway—it is built into the side of a small rise in the land, giving it the look of a bunker more than a family dwelling. In an area where houses are built with peaked roofs as protection against the weight of heavy winter snowfalls, its flat roof gives this one an unfinished appearance, as if a second story was planned but never built.

In contrast to the ugliness of the house itself, Wynkoop Lane is a picturesque country road situated a few miles east of the village of Rhinebeck and reached by one of the several two-lane highways that provide access to the surrounding countryside. As one travels up the road, the houses get larger, and the land around them is counted in acres instead of feet. But even in the low-rent district down near the highway, there's plenty of room for children to roam, for the forest is their back yard.

In the world of business, the senior Goetz's Teutonic temperament—the commitment to discipline, the sense of order, the certainty, the confidence in his destiny—served him well. But the same qualities expressed in the family, which he ran like a Prussian general, made for difficult times for his wife and children. Indeed, he was an interesting paradox, this man. A humanist concerned for the oppressed peoples of the world, he could be cruel in the extreme to those closest to him.

The portrait of young Bernie drawn by those who knew him then already reflects the contradictions and conflicts that would characterize Bernie Goetz in his later years. The splits the world would eventually come to know—the timid, law-abiding good citizen and the gun-toting subway vigilante; the man torn between a deep desire for privacy while he basks in the public notice—were evident even as a small child.

On the one hand, he's pictured as having been a shy, quiet, very good little boy, always serious beyond his years, a child who could be happy playing by himself for hours at a time. It was as if, even at three, he knew, as children always seem to know, that he dared not be responsible for one more burden on his parents, that his welcome in the family depended upon his being good. "When he was a little kid, he would be happy for an afternoon if you would give him old leaves, old bugs and a magnifying glass," sister Barbara tells a reporter for *Newsday*, a suburban New York newspaper.

On the other hand, the same sister says also that he would follow his older siblings around, hounding them for their attention, and that he could be audaciously rash and uncontrollable at times. So, for example, once, when he was told to be quiet, he climbed a tree and urinated on an aunt below, arguing afterwards that he had, after all, followed instructions. He had been quiet.

Both parents were strict, the children agree, but it was their father's arbitrary expectations and dictatorial ways that made their mark. "The father was very stern, a real Prussian disciplinarian," an aunt tells the same *Newsday* reporter. "He was very strict with the boys, much stricter with the boys than with the girls. He was too dictatorial—what the father decrees, that's law. . . . Affectionate? No, he was a cold fish."

Cold and cruel, especially to his sons, who were defenseless against this father who, time and again, humbled and humiliated them with his words, his deeds and his hands. "He pushed them too hard," says his elder daughter sadly. But no matter what suffering he might inflict upon them, there was no one to intervene. Gertrude Goetz, loving mother though she was, could not stand up to her husband in defense of her children. She remained the passive, obedient wife, no matter what the provocation. And Bernhard Goetz reigned the undisputed master of the house.

When a child failed the senior Goetz's expectations, he would roar with rage, frightening the entire household with his bluster, recalls Barbara. He would demand that the offender put in writing what he called a "memorandum of understanding"—a letter demonstrating that his expectations were understood and promising that there would be no recurrence of the infraction. In one such letter, young Bernie, aged eleven, wrote to his father:

Dear Mr. Goetz,
   I am sorry I've been a bad boy. I will be good from now on. I won't yell, write on the walls, and make a lot of noise. I will pay attention, I won't jump around, and I'll do what mother tells me.
                                        Your son,
                                        Bernhard Goetz

Outside the house, Bernie seemed to all who knew him to be a sweet, pleasant child—well mannered, never causing any trouble. "The boy was always real quiet, like a mouse, hardly knew he was around," recalls a neighbor. But he must also have been lonely. "He never really had a friend the whole time he was growing up, leastways not as far as I could tell," says another.

In the family, sister Barbara and brother George were already half grown, not likely candidates for playmates. Only Bernice was nearer in age—about two years older. They were emotionally close, these two younger children, almost a separate family from their older siblings, so wide was the age disparity. But Bernice was an active, outgoing girl, not likely to be hanging around the house with nothing to do or looking to her little brother for company.

In a school where there were just over fifty children who started kindergarten together and where forty-eight of them graduated from the town's high school, everyone knew who young Bernhard was. "But," says a woman who sat near him from kindergarten through sixth grade, "I don't know what I can tell you about him; he was like a shadow. He was there, but you couldn't talk to him. You never saw him talking to anyone or playing with anyone. All I remember about him is that he always had his nose in a book. I don't think anybody even noticed when he left our school. I know I didn't. I think it must have been after the sixth grade because his picture isn't in the yearbook after that."

The same stories are told repeatedly. Bernie was quiet and smart, not disliked, but not liked either, remembered, yet not known. One man who rode the school bus with him daily for six years says, "It's real hard to remember anything specific about him. He was just there, but he was never part of anything, either on the bus or off it, like the other kids. You know how kids form groups? Well, he didn't ever belong to any group of kids. I can still picture him all alone. I never remember him talking to anyone at all."

But he wasn't always left alone. With no circle of friends within which to hide or to gain some protection from the cruelty of other children, he became a safe and easy target for their aggressions. "The other kids would tease him and hit him. I don't know why, maybe because he was so very bright," says one of Bernie's grade-school teachers. "But he hated any kind of fighting and would shy away when problems came up. And that made them go after him even more. I used to feel so sorry for him; he went home crying so often."

"He was always the butt of jokes and teasing," a schoolmate remembers. "You know how very cruel kids can be. Sometimes he'd run away, and other times he just stood there and took it, never said a word. But inside I'm sure the pressure was just building and building."

In between such adventures, he was paid no mind. Another classmate describes Bernie's relationship to the other children quite graphically. "If you were painting a picture of the school scene, you'd have some of the students out in front and some in the background. Maybe you'd remember their names because it was a small school in a small town, but that would be all. Well, that's the way he was—in the background. So most of the time you didn't see him then, and now you can't hardly remember anything about him. Christ, his name didn't even register with me when I read it in the papers. It wasn't until someone said to me, 'Hey, did you see what old Bernie Goetz did?' that I put it together."

One man, now a respected businessman in the community, re-calls Bernie with an odd combination of regret and glee that's probably not much different from what he felt as a boy. "You know how rough kids can be on each other. When we paid attention to him at all, he got teased. He was an oddball, didn't mix well; he didn't fit, if you know what I mean, a real loner.

"And coordination-wise, he didn't develop like the rest of us. Even as a kid, I felt kind of sorry for him. But"—laughing as the memories of those school days so many years ago return—"if

I was to characterize him, it would be like that cartoon character Goofy—you know, if somebody was going to drop something or trip over his feet, it would be Bernie. In gym class, well, you didn't want him on your baseball team. When we'd choose up sides, he'd be the last kid picked. And if you got stuck with him, you'd put him out in right field and tell him to hug the line and stay out of your way."

For young Bernie, loneliness and humiliation were piled one on top of the other. Schoolmates and teachers remember feeling sorry for him as they watched him stand always on the sidelines. Neighbors recount vividly how often he came home in tears. "I'd see him come running home from school crying so often that sometimes I'd think to myself: 'Why can't you learn to stand up for yourself and fight?' But most of the time, I just felt very sorry for him; he was such a slight, puny little kid with his face streaked with tears."

Tears of pain and humiliation, certainly, and tears of helpless rage as well. Eventually, he will learn to stop the crying, but the feelings—the remembrance of the shame and the rage— will not be erased so readily.

9. Long before anyone knows who the gunman is, he emerges as a human being in the press reports, a man whose fear is comprehensible, whose rage finds its match in our own hearts. He is one of us. But the youths he shot are strangers, alien creatures beyond our understanding.

There are four of them, yet they seem always to be lumped together as one, as if discriminating among them is impossible. They are faceless and formless, Ralph Ellison's *Invisible Man*. In the media as well as on the streets, they are seen as hoodlums, punks, thugs, subway marauders.

The enemy dehumanized—just as in a war. It justified our slaughter of the Indians, the Turks' massacre of the Armenians, Stalin's murder of his political enemies, Hitler's extermination of the Jews. It is this that made our soldiers' behavior at My Lai possible. And it is also the mark of our urban wars today. "Don't talk to me about them; they're not people. They're animals; they belong in a jungle," spits out the manager of a supermarket on New York's Upper East Side when told that two of the youths were shot in the back. "I don't give a damn where he shot them. If you ask me, the man's a saint. We should give him some extra bullets, extra guns and a year's supply of tokens and turn him loose on the subways."

The portrait of Bernie Goetz is presented to us in full living color; the one of the youths is a flat black-and-white. Goetz becomes a many-faceted, complex human being; they are stereotypes. We know how tall he is, how slight his build, the color of his hair and eyes, what kind of glasses he wears, what clothes he prefers. All things that make him seem life-size, human.

But the young men who were shot lie in their hospital beds, the reviled actors in this latest national morality play. We hear nothing about their physical characteristics, about the clothes they wear. We don't know that Darrell is a dapper dresser, that James prefers army fatigues. We have no idea whether one is better-looking, more appealing than another; whether one is shy and another bold. We don't even know how well they knew each other before they came together on that Saturday afternoon.

No one tells us, either, that they're all slight of build, more so than Bernie Goetz. And much shorter than his five feet ten as well. At about five-six, James is the tallest; the other three hover around five-four. Without these facts, our imaginations are left to work overtime, as we picture four huge blacks menacing this one small, lone white man.

It's a more interesting story told that way, of course, its dramatic possibilities enhanced by the image of one honorable man pitted against four brawny, evil thugs. And in this age of sensation, the media must keep the drama high if they're to hold our attention. But it's also more than that. It's a story of heroes and villains that gives legitimacy to our rage and reinforces our righteousness. So, time and again, the media play their parts, albeit not always consciously—television, radio, and the press all reflecting back to us the story as they know we want and need to hear it.

As soon as Goetz's identity becomes known, reporters do a splendid job of investigating his past and telling his life story to the world. We hear repeatedly, for example, that he was mugged by three black youths a few years ago. As such personal assaults have become more common in our society, we have learned that while the physical trauma may heal quickly, the emotional impact leaves invisible wounds that take longer to knit. So it doesn't surprise us when we read that Bernie never got over his fear of being hurt again, and that he was carrying an unlicensed gun to protect himself against another such assault.

We're told in great detail about how his attackers jumped him as he entered the subway station at Canal Street one afternoon, about how he fled up the steps with the three men in pursuit, about how they wrested from him the expensive electronic equipment he was carrying, about how he was injured when they beat him and threw him against a plate-glass window, about how that injury has left him with some permanent damage to the cartilage in his chest.

Fortunately for him, a policeman appeared on the scene, frightening off two of his assailants. The third was apprehended. But, much to Bernie's disgust, the perpetrator of the crime was held at police headquarters for only two hours and thirty-five minutes, while he, Goetz, was detained for six hours and five minutes—apparently part of the procedures necessary for him to file charges. Even though his attacker eventually pleaded guilty to a misdemeanor assault charge and was sentenced to six months, Goetz has remained dissatisfied with the way the police handled the case and with its outcome.

Although it's three years since that mugging, he's still angry at what he sees as the incompetence and inequities of the criminal justice system, the stories tell us—a rage that burned ever more brightly when his request for a gun permit was denied a short time later. "They told me: 'We can't give a pistol permit to everybody who wants one. That would be irresponsible.' The incident was an education. It taught me that the city doesn't care what happens to you. . . . They don't know what it's like to be a victim."

The word pictures the news stories draw are vivid. So whether we've been mugged or not is irrelevant; our imaginations fill in for experience. Therefore, even if we didn't understand before, by the time we're finished reading these accounts, Bernie Goetz becomes a person with whom we can empathize. This is a man whose motives we can comprehend, a man whose internal states at the moment of confrontation we can share.

But there's little in the press reports that makes it possible for us to take an empathic step toward Barry Allen, Darrell Cabey, Troy Canty and James Ramseur, nothing to help us understand what might have hurt, frightened or enraged them. About them, we read only the same bare story over and over again: They're eighteen and nineteen, high-school dropouts, unemployed, live in the South Bronx, have long criminal records. Nothing to discriminate among them, nothing to indicate that their "long criminal records" are quite a bit longer for some than for others, or that the crimes on the record are a lot more petty than the words imply. And weeks after it has been fully repudiated, some of the most respected crime reporters in the city are still writing that they were carrying sharpened screwdrivers.

It isn't that the people who write these stories mean to distort the truth. But if these youths are the enemy—the embodiment of every black kid who ever made us shrink in fear— anything is possible, anything believable. In a perfectly human psychological maneuver, therefore, these reporters, too, attend selectively to the facts that come across their desks, allowing into consciousness those that fit their already existing beliefs, screening out those that contravene them. To do otherwise would be to risk humanizing the foe and, ultimately, to have to put an end to war.

So on December 31, the same day, not far from the same hour when the man who shot him is surrendering in New Hampshire, Barry Allen goes home after nine days of hospitalization. An interesting human-interest note in a very big story. Yet it gets buried on the inside pages with no comment about this conjunction of events. No comment either about how wan he looks after nine days in the hospital, about the fact that he's even skinnier than usual but still an attractive young man.

Two days later, on January 2, Bernhard Goetz is arraigned in a New Hampshire court while Troy Canty is preparing to leave the hospital. The next day the New York *Post* publishes two pictures on its front page. On the left is Bernie—white, blond, sensitive, head down, a pensive look on his face, hand-cuffed and surrounded by police. On the right is Troy—black, arrogant, arms folded across his chest, eyes hooded, belligerent, free. In between the photographs is the headline: "Led Away in Cuffs While Wounded Mugger Walks to Freedom." No con-straint about the use of the word "mugger," not even the tradi-tional "alleged" to modify the charge, just the word "mugger," as if it were a fact already proven.

James Ramseur and Darrell Cabey, who were hit with hollow-point bullets, are still in the hospital. James, listed in satisfactory condition at Bellevue Hospital, will remain there until January 12, three full weeks from the time he was wounded. Darrell is in critical condition at St. Vincent's, paralyzed from the waist down and trying to fight off the threat of pneumonia. But we don't read or hear much about them—at least not until January 9, when Darrell loses his fight, stops breathing and slips into a coma. Then it becomes big news. If he dies, Bernhard Goetz may be charged with murder.

10 · New York City is caught up in a euphoria only rarely seen in this city that prides itself on its cool cynicism. "God Bless You, Bernie," the signs all over town cry out. Speaking the sentiments of millions of others, a letter to the New York *Post* exults, "Yes, Virginia, there is a Santa Claus—and he lives on 14th Street."

There are fourteen thousand crimes a year on New York's subways, thirty-eight every day, most of them by youths who live in one or another of the city's ghettoes. That's only 2.6 percent of the crimes in the city, the politicians remind New Yorkers from time to time, suggesting that the streets are more dangerous than the subways. But it's an argument that cuts little ice with the weary citizens of this city. "The point is," says a Brooklyn woman who works in Manhattan, "I don't *have* to go out on the streets late at night, but I have to ride the subway; it's the only way I can get to work."

Still it's true that this subway system, which runs daily around the clock, carries one billion riders a year, about 3.5 million a day. In that context, thirty-eight crimes doesn't seem so much, especially to those who have never ridden a New York subway. But for the people who live and work there, it's another story. "Don't talk to me about your lousy statistics," another subway rider fumes. "Everyone's scared to go down there because you never know what's going to happen."

"Down there"—under the ground where the cleansing, healing sun never shines, where the air is fetid and people are jammed in with scarcely any room to breathe, trapped like rats in a cage. "Down there"—where life seems even more unpredictable than in the world above, where the ancient system breaks down too often, where in one month alone last year there were 465 track fires that caused agonizing and sometimes dangerous delays, where the lighting is so bad in one out of five cars that reading is difficult, where blackouts occur with increasing frequency, where you never know who's standing next to you and what he might do.

There are some large crimes in this world under the ground—thefts, muggings, stabbings, murders. But mostly it's the small harassments and humiliations that make daily life a misery for those who must ride the subways—a push here, a shove there, a blaring radio, an intimidating posture, a taunting stare. And the graffiti, especially the graffiti, an assault on the senses from which there's no escape. "Why would anyone want to deface public property like that?" we ask wonderingly, not really expecting an answer that will satisfy.

Seeming unfeeling and uncaring, some small number of youths take spray paint to the walls and windows of the subways. They're the same kids who walk into a train as if they own it, by their very posture telegraphing a message that says, "You're on my turf now, and I'll do with it and you what I want." They remind us that we are a society divided by race, that there's a menacing presence in our midst that we cannot fully control. If their intent is to frighten us, to tap our anxiety about our helplessness, they succeed. If they mean to make us face the hatred that lives inside us, they accomplish their purpose well.

But at least for a little while after the shootings, people walk more confidently, feel more self-assured, even in the subways. So when, at the height of the morning rush hour less than two weeks later, a boy boards an uptown IRT express with the volume of his large portable stereo on high, people don't seethe silently but ineffectually as they have until now. Instead, a new script is played out.

It's just before eight o'clock when the train pulls into the Fourteenth Street station—the same one from which Bernie Goetz entered the subway on that fateful Saturday twelve days ago. As the doors are about to close, a Puerto Rican youth, about sixteen years old, sprints through the door, elbows his way through the crowd until he reaches one of the posts people hold on to for support, and, taking up more than his share of the scarce space, leans against the pole and listens to the music as the train careens along.

It's a common occurrence, even though there's a law in New York prohibiting the playing of these radios on the subway. But who is there to enforce the law? Certainly not the passengers, who usually suffer the noise wordlessly, even while they may feel assaulted by it, may be furious inside.

On this day, however, without a word, one pair of eyes turns toward the culprit, then another, and another. An odd silence fills the car, a silence that rises above the noise. Women and men all around turn their eyes on the boy until he's surrounded by people glaring at him, a wordless challenge, a silent demand that he turn that damn thing off. He shifts his feet uncomfortably, hitches his jeans, tries for a while to pay no attention.

No one says a word, but people seem to draw closer together, made stronger by the strength of their unspoken resolve. *This is a fight they will win.* Another moment or two go by, then with a shrug the boy reaches down and snaps off the radio.

For the first time, the people in the car look at each other and smile; a sense of unity binds them. We did it! We won! One man lifts a fist in triumph; a woman gives the thumbs-up sign. Collectively they heave a satisfied sigh. No word has been spoken among them; no need for words. They all know that together they won one.

Bernie Goetz, it seems, has given uncounted Americans a sense of possibility once again, allowed them to believe once more in their efficacy, returned to them the hope that they can regain control in a world that seems to have gone mad. Powerful forces have been let loose inside the American people—forces for good, to be sure, and forces for evil as well. But few want to think about evil right now, at least not about the evil that might lie inside them. They're feeling too good.

11· 1973—the first time Shirley Cabey got a call from the police telling her that catastrophe had struck her family. She, her husband and their five sons were living in the downstairs four-bedroom apartment of a two-family house in Far Rockaway, just a short stroll from the beach. Summer or winter, it was a good place to raise children. Even when it was too cold to go in the water, the children liked to play in the sand, to listen to the sound of the ocean, to watch in wonder its winter fury as the waves came crashing against the shore.

When they didn't go to the beach, Darrell* and his brothers could still play outside while Mrs. Cabey did her work inside. The house had both a front and a back yard—plenty of space for the kids to roam with their beloved dog Flocko and still remain under a mother's watchful eye. If they wandered off a bit, she didn't worry; it was a nice street, safe, with open fields nearby.

These were good times, no riches, but they all had what they needed. Ronald Cabey was working, driving a truck, making

---

* Among family and friends, Darrell is known as Gene, short for Eugene, his middle name. To avoid confusion, however, I shall refer to him as Darrell throughout, since that is how he has been known to the public since he was wounded. Even his mother now calls him Darrell when talking about him to anyone other than family and close friends.

good wages. There was plenty of food on the table, nice clothes for the kids, two cars, enough money so they could take an occasional vacation, entertain family and friends fairly often, and get a babysitter and go out on the town once in a while.

There were some problems in the marriage, as in all marriages. They would get angry at each other, have a fight, maybe not speak for days, even talk about separating sometimes. But eventually things would get peaceful between them again. They both knew it wasn't perfect, but they also appreciated what they had. A relatively solid marriage, partners who, underneath whatever their struggles, liked and respected each other most of the time. She was a good wife and loving mother; he was a good provider. Together they made a good team. It was a lot more than either of their parents ever had, a lot more than others around them could count. Stability, respectability and soon, the American dream—a business of his own.

When his boss decided to retire, Mr. Cabey bought one of the trucks and struck out on his own. He worked harder than ever after that; it seemed like he was working all the time. The kids missed him, but he tried to make it up to them when he came home at night. Sometimes, when he worked real late, Darrell and his older brother wouldn't let themselves fall asleep until they knew he had come in. Their world felt complete then, safe.

Then without warning, it all collapsed. Ronald Cabey was dead. He had gone into a diner to get something to eat, leaving his truck in one of the parking spaces right in front of the window where he could see it. Before he put the first bite in his mouth, he looked out to see someone easing his truck out of its space. He raced outside, jumped on the running board and, hanging on to the driver's side, wrestled with the man in the cab. The thief pulled a gun, but that didn't deter Cabey. This was his living, his life, his dream come true. He couldn't let it go without a fight. So he hung on as if for life itself. And it cost him his life.

Trying to shake Cabey off, the driver swerved the truck sharply as he turned out of the driveway and into the street. At just that moment a car was turning into the lot and came alongside. Too close. Ronald Cabey was caught and crushed between the two vehicles. His stolen truck sped off as he lay dying in the street.

Shirley Cabey, married at sixteen, widowed at twenty-six, her children, ranging in age from two to nine, left fatherless. A native New Yorker, Mrs. Cabey was raised by her mother alone after her parents separated when she was a very small girl. Now she would have to raise her own children alone as well.

Terrified, feeling lost and abandoned, she worried about what would become of them. In the initial shock of her husband's death, it was hard even to imagine how she would manage. She couldn't work with five small kids. But if she didn't, who would support them? She knew they couldn't stay in the house in Far Rockaway. But where would they live? She and her husband had saved some money, but not much, not enough to last more than a few months no matter how careful she might be.

She was so besieged with questions and concerns, she hardly had time to mourn properly. At night, when she could finally lie down in the bed they had shared, she lay achingly, frighteningly alone, her eyes wide open, her heart so full of anxiety, her head so full of the endless stream of worries that poured through her, there was no room for tears.

In time, it got sorted out. Social security payments for the children, along with food stamps, helped. And there were the projects. She hated to leave her nice, safe house, was terrified when she heard she'd be living on the twenty-first floor. Twenty-one floors up! She had nightmares about a child falling out of a window. But she had no choice. So she moved and, winter or summer, kept the windows locked tight while the children were small.

It took a while for all of them to get used to living in Claremont Village. Every time she wanted to take the baby out for some air, every time the older ones wanted to go out to play, she had to get all five kids dressed and ready to go. It was exhausting and aggravating, chasing after first one child and then another. Yet she couldn't let them either stay in or go out alone.

Once she got outside her apartment, she never knew what she'd find. The narrow halls in the building were so filthy, she was afraid to let a child touch anything. The elevator smelled so awful, she wanted to hold her breath all the way down. And the streets—the torment of every parent in the project. How would she keep the kids off those streets?

For the children, too, it meant dealing with a whole new way of life at the same time they were struggling to adapt to the loss of their father. It wasn't long before Mrs. Cabey began to see signs of trouble and sought help. "After my husband was killed, I worried about all the kids, especially the one just behind Darrell. Y'know how kids are; they can't talk about things that hurt them so easy. So I went with the whole family to counseling. It helped, I think, kind of settled them down."

But not for long. As Darrell advanced through his teenage years, the streets made their claim. He was small, five feet four, and slight—not easy for any teenage boy in our society, less so for a kid who had to make his way on the streets of the project, where the law is that you "either lick 'em or join 'em."

He was angry, too, although he rarely allowed it to show. What was the use? Besides, he knew it would make his mother unhappy. He didn't want her to think he was complaining or something; it wasn't her fault. So he hid behind an impassive exterior while the rage boiled unexpressed inside him—a rage that had simmered in him since his father was killed when he was seven years old.

He remembered his father, but he couldn't talk about him; it was too hard, hurt too much. He was afraid, also, that if he did, he'd never be able to contain the anger. But inside, he thought about him, sometimes even cried silently. Why'd they have to kill him? Bastards! Goddamn dirty bastards!

The past with its pain, the present with its dangers, the future that looked so empty, all combined to loosen the grip of family and school until, early in 1984, Darrell Cabey walked out of his eleventh-grade classroom and ended his school career. "I tried to keep him in school, the good Lord knows I tried. But what can you do when all the kids are dropping out?" his mother now cries helplessly.

"We just got tired of goin' t' school," explains his longtime best friend, Lydell, who dropped out with Darrell. "I don't know why we did it; we just did; maybe to get a job or somethin'."

Shirley Cabey was disturbed about Darrell. But knowing she was powerless to change what she saw, she kept telling herself that it was only temporary, that he'd soon find himself, that the boy who, she insists, "never gave me no trouble" would emerge once more. So when, a little while later, her son became involved with a nice girl and began to work more steadily at his part-time job bagging groceries in a market in Harlem, she was eager to be reassured.

She was proud of the fact that Darrell, always a sharp dresser, grew even more concerned about his appearance. "He always dressed real nice, and when he got this girlfriend, Denise, he took real special care, taking a shower every day. I always liked to look at him when he was going out to see her," his mother recalls with pride, unshed tears now glistening in her eyes. She remembers, also, watching the two of them together and thinking happily: "Maybe now he'll stop staying out so late; maybe he'll even go back to school."

But that hope was shattered when Denise left Darrell and he began the downward spiral that would put him on the #2 IRT downtown express that fateful afternoon in December. After that, she knew even less than before about where he was, what he was doing, or who he was doing it with. "I felt there was something going on, but I didn't know exactly what it was. I was worried when he was spending so much time away from home, and I tried to talk to him; it just wasn't any use. He was never much of a talker, but then he wouldn't hardly say anything. Sometimes I'd wonder if he even heard me. Mind you, he was always polite and respectful and very considerate, but it was like he couldn't hear me."

After his breakup with Denise, Darrell became more of a regular among the tough young men who hung out on the corner of Washington and Third. As his friend Lydell tells it, Darrell would urge him to come along as he prepared to join some of the other guys on the street in one hustle or another. But somehow Lydell was wise enough to be afraid. "He'd tell me, 'C'mon, Lydell, let's go,' but I'd say, 'No way I'm goin' to go with y'all.' I knew they were up to trouble. I just wished I could've made him see it like I did. But Darrell, he couldn't say no, just couldn't do it."

Although there were no convictions on his record, by the time of the shootings Darrell had already come to the attention of the local police several times. Twice they had served him with a summons for blocking pedestrian traffic in the stairwell of one of the buildings in the project. Once he and some others were found in the community center of a building and charged with burglary. All misdemeanors. And just two months before the shootings, a Bronx grand jury handed up an indictment against Darrell for armed robbery, a felony he insisted he didn't commit.

By this time, too, he already had had an occasional involvement in the popular ghetto pastime of breaking into video-game machines and extracting the change. Drugs, epidemic in the project, also began to take their toll. He smoked weed, snorted coke, ingested angel dust. But given the quality of the street drugs in these ghettoes, who knows what he put up his nose or into his stomach and lungs?

Some days he was so stoned he didn't know where he was, could hardly remember his name. "I used to call him 'Space Face,' 'cause you could be talkin' and talkin' and all of a sudden you'd know he didn't hear anythin' you been sayin'," Lydell remembers sadly. He tells of the day he came upon Darrell sporting a deep cut on his head. "He told me, 'Man, I must've tripped on the sidewalk or somethin' last night.' " But Lydell knew differently. He had already heard some of the others on the street bragging about how they had waited until Darrell got high, then robbed him. "So I told him, 'Man, you didn't trip on no sidewalk; they picked you up and threw you down on the ground.' But he was so out of it, he couldn't hardly know what I was sayin', and he didn't feel no pain 'til the next day."

Darrell knew he was in trouble, tried sometimes to pull himself together, but it was hard to care enough to stop himself. Sometimes he would hear his mother's voice deep inside him, talking to him, begging him, warning him. But it wasn't enough.

In the week before he was shot, he went to stay at his grandmother's house. She was sick and, with his mother working, he volunteered to stay with her until she got better. Grasping at anything that might signify that the boy she used to know was still alive and well, Mrs. Cabey took comfort in this sign of his caring concern. "Darrell was always very helpful, affectionate, too. Just before he got hurt, my mother got the flu and he stayed over at her house and took care of her."

Her nagging worries about Darrell abated for the first time in months. "He was still there that Friday night before he got shot, so even if I would've been worried about him then, I never would've dreamed it was Darrell when I heard on the TV that four kids had been shot on the subway way down in Manhattan."

Late on the morning of Saturday, December 22, Darrell left

his grandmother's house and wandered around the streets aimlessly, looking for something—some company, some action, a score, anything to relieve the emptiness, the hopelessness inside him. He started toward home, decided against it and changed direction, heading instead to the corner, where he knew at least that "somethin's always happenin'."

At about the same time, Troy Canty, Barry Allen and James Ramseur were also making their separate ways through the streets of the project, each of them heading without much thought to the favored meeting place. As far as anyone knows, none of the boys were ever close friends. Some of them knew each other before that day, some didn't. Darrell knew Barry and James vaguely, but he'd never seen Troy before.

There was nothing to do out there on the corner. And even if there had been, no one had any money to do anything with. James had a screwdriver in his pocket; Darrell had two—the tools of their trade, carried with them often, just in case. Altogether they had only three among the four of them, but they figured they'd manage. "Hey, man, what we hangin' here for? Let's go downtown and pick up some bread," one of them said. Which one? It makes no difference who said the words; the thought was there for all of them.

A few minutes later, they jumped the turnstiles at the subway station and boarded the #2 IRT downtown express.

12 · Now that he's in custody, a picture begins to emerge that makes Bernhard Goetz seem even more appealing, more like an ordinary guy than anyone had imagined. From his jail cell in New Hampshire comes word that he's frightened and deeply depressed. "He seems to be scared all the time. He's a nice quiet fellow; he's very polite and minds his own business. But I don't think he got much sleep that first night they brought him in," reports an observer.

A fellow inmate tells reporters that Bernie was housed in the "rubber room," jailhouse parlance for the padded cell. He spent most of the time, this jail mate says, hiding in the corner with a blanket over his head. "A guard asked if I had any shaving cream for him, and when I approached him and began to talk to him, he thought I was going to hit him. He covered up a bit and became real frightened."

The Concord police, however, have a different and more complex reading of Bernie Goetz, reporting that he would be talking and joking one minute, serious and thoughtful the next and, just as suddenly, withdrawn and angry. Police Chief David Walchak says, "He's an extremely complicated and very erratic guy. All you have to do is look at how he's behaved around here. He changes his mind from one day to the next. He says he won't have a lawyer. Then all of a sudden, he's got one. One day he tells us he won't go for extradition; he'll fight it. Then the next day in court he says, 'Sure I'll go to New York.' He insists he doesn't want any publicity and that he won't talk to us if we talk to the press. Then he does all these things that are guaranteed to get press attention."

After two days of contradictory statements about whether he'll return voluntarily or will force the State of New York to seek his extradition, he agrees to come back. On January 3, following a dramatic high-speed ride down the interstate with the press in hot pursuit, he's brought back to a hero's welcome in the city.

Not long after his arrival, he's led into a packed courtroom for his arraignment—250 people all trying to get a look at this new celebrity. What they see is an unshaven, confused-looking man, his hands cuffed before him. He's wearing jeans, a light plaid shirt and a reddish-brown leather jacket with a fur collar.

Frank Brenner, a former judge, is appointed by the court to represent him. Throughout the short proceedings, Goetz seems distracted, unable to fix his attention on the happenings before him for more than a moment at a time. Occasionally he mumbles something to himself, as if responding to some conversation no one else can hear.

During the hearing, Assistant DA Susan Braver presents the facts as Bernie Goetz has told them in New Hampshire. He shot two people in the back, she tells the court, "striking them as they were moving away in the opposite direction. Then he fired a fifth time at one who was not yet down. By his own admission, he intended to shoot each one of them. He only stopped because he ran out of ammunition."

When the hearing is over, Bernhard Goetz has been arraigned

on four charges of attempted murder and a weapons charge, and sent to Rikers Island in lieu of $50,000 bail, the amount requested by the district attorney. While acceding to the DA's request, Judge Leslie Snyder, herself a former prosecutor, is sufficiently nonplussed to remark, "This is a low bail request by the people. I'm surprised. If Western civilization has taught us anything, it is that we cannot tolerate individuals taking law and justice into their own hands."

But this court will have nothing further to say in the matter. The case will now be presented to the grand jury. It's this panel of twenty-three New Yorkers who will decide whether a crime has been committed, whether Bernie Goetz took justice into his own hands.

The details of the shootings presented in court by the district attorney are the first to be made public. Yet they go relatively unnoticed. All three of New York City's major newspapers report the story only partially; all bury it in headlines that trumpet the news of the $50,000 bail.

The *Post*, always the most dramatic, screams: "New Yorkers in Pledge to Aid Vigilante." But even the *Times* reports the day's events in court under a headline that reads: "Goetz Held at Rikers I. in $50,000 Bail in Wounding of 4 Teen-Agers on IRT." No focus on the fact that two of the youths were shot in the back; nothing to draw attention to his having taken a second shot at one of them, not even to the fact that this was the bullet that turned Darrell Cabey into a lifelong cripple.

No one asks either what Bernie was thinking when he boarded that train and sat down in the middle of four black teenagers with no one else around when there were twenty or more passengers at the other end of the car. New Yorkers agree that, when they walk into a subway car, they look around for what they hope will be a safe place to sit. Anyone, whether a weary

and worldly-wise city resident or a naïve tourist, seeing four
noisy black kids at one end of the train and a couple of dozen
ordinary-looking types at the other end, would move in the
latter direction for a seat. "Nobody gets on the subway without
watching what's happening around you," says an experienced
rider. "You pick the seat you're going to sit in, and you pick
a place or a person that seems safe. It's not so much that you
think about it and plan it. If you ride the subways every day
like I do, it's something automatic, like looking both ways
before you cross the street."

"It makes no sense," says one of Bernie's neighbors as he
reflects on the situation, "especially since he was mugged once
and really was afraid about it happening again." He pauses to
consider the words he has just spoken: "At least it seemed like he
was. I was mugged on the subway a few years ago, and you can
bet your bottom dollar I've been on guard ever since. I wouldn't
have sat down anywhere near them if I had a choice. Not unless
I was looking for trouble and knew I had the means to win the
fight."

Officials in Concord, meanwhile, watch in wonder. Referring
to the difference between the $500,000 bail set in his juris-
diction and the $50,000 bail in New York, Chief Walchak
comments acidly, "I hope that lives aren't $450,000 cheaper in
New York than they are in New Hampshire. . . . Bernhard
Goetz is no innocent good guy who was just defending himself,"
he warns. "He's a very complicated human being who's also a
dangerous one."

Andrew Isaac, the Assistant Attorney General who drew up
the complaint in New Hampshire, says that, based on the evidence he has seen, "there are indications of premeditation," and
that he sees nothing "that would excuse [Goetz's] use of deadly
force."

Chief Walchak explains, "When I say it's not self-defense, I mean he probably was scared; there probably were some overt actions to which he reacted violently. But it's like asking the question 'When does spanking turn into child abuse?' Well, it's the same thing here. 'When does self-defense turn into attempted murder?' In this case, I think we know the answer up here.

"In my view, he had a propensity for this type of situation and had predetermined that if he was ever accosted again, he'd take action. He's very erratic. I don't mean his emotions weren't in control when he shot those guys, or that he didn't know what he was doing. He knew all right, but there's something very erratic, very dangerous about him."

Immediately after the arraignment proceedings, five men who say they're friends and associates hold a press conference outside the courthouse to announce the establishment of the Bernhard Goetz Legal Defense Fund. Curtis Sliwa, head of the Guardian Angels, is named an honorary member after he donates $102 which he solicited from subway riders the night before. Attorney Serphin Maltese, executive director of the state Conservative Party, announces that fund co-chairman Bernard Goldstein has asked him to serve as Goetz's counsel.

People from all walks of life call and write to say they want to aid in Goetz's defense. As many as forty envelopes a day, all stuffed with cash and checks, are left in the Defense Fund box in the lobby of his apartment building. A boy in Seattle empties his piggy bank; a retired railroad worker in Atlanta offers part of his pension; a farmer in South Dakota pledges $2,000. From Los Angeles, Joan Rivers sends words of admiration along with the promise of money for his bail. The sheriff of Lumpkin County in Georgia tells the world he's raising money for Bernie's defense. "I'm glad to see someone who's got enough guts to stand up for his rights," he says. In Goetz's home state, Re-

publican Party chairman George Clark, saying that he's "scared
of some of the creatures" on the city's subways, announces that
he's willing to put up $5,000 of his own money to help.

From Rikers Island, Bernie refuses all offers from both the
public and his family, vowing to stay in jail until he can make
bail himself. Admiration for him rises; the Goetz cult grows.
People shake their heads, unbelieving: with all the freeloaders
in the world, this guy asks for nothing, will accept nothing.

On Monday, January 7, his brother George, an engineer in
Detroit, and his sister Bernice, manager of the family's real
estate development firm, now located in Florida, fly to New
York to talk with Bernie. They arrive at the jail carrying a black
attaché case and two plastic shopping bags. Asked by reporters
if he brought the $50,000 for his brother's bail, George only
smiles and says, "I've been told by the attorney not to discuss
that."

For the first time, we learn that making his own bail will be
no problem for Bernie. He's independently wealthy, his father
having died earlier in the year and left a considerable estate to
be divided among his four children.

After a two-hour private visit, the two siblings emerge smiling
and animated. "He's in very good spirits and he's doing well,"
Bernice tells the press. No one talks about whether bail has been
made. But a statement by a prison spokesman leaves room for
no other inference. Bernie probably won't leave for a day or
two, he announces, because "he's afraid to be out on the streets.
He feels safer where he is."

Late the next afternoon, six days after he was sent to Rikers,
Bernie Goetz is released under a cloak of secrecy. Edward
Hershey of the city's Department of Correction says that Bernie's
bail was paid with personal funds and that, at his request, he was
released quietly because he was concerned about his safety. His

court-appointed attorney, Frank Brenner, is caught by surprise. "I don't know why he did it. I didn't know about it."

The next morning, a smiling Bernie makes a brief appearance in Criminal Court, just long enough to hear the district attorney's office request a postponement of a scheduled hearing because they're still presenting evidence to the grand jury. Outside, Bernie thanks New Yorkers for their support. "Thank you! Thank you!" he shouts at the crowds who greet him. "All I can say is that things are a little hectic now, but I'm looking forward to being home."

In one of those ironic collisions of events that have marked this whole case, at about the time Bernie is accepting the plaudits of the crowd, Darrell Cabey is falling into a coma. It's unclear now if he'll ever go home again.

By now, Bernie Goetz and the subway shootings are the subject of conversation wherever and whenever people come together. A Washington *Post*–ABC News public opinion poll taken in mid-January reports that 86 percent of those interviewed nationally know about New York's subway gunman. In the eastern region of the country alone, the proportion rises to 95 percent—a level of public attention and awareness that isn't given to most major national events, not to a presidential election, not even to the Iranian hostage crisis, which dominated the news for 444 straight days a few years ago. A few weeks later, a Roper poll comparing the public recognition of Bernie Goetz and New York's Governor Mario Cuomo, widely touted as the next Democratic candidate for the presidency, shows that twice as many people have heard of Bernie.

Talk-show hosts from coast to coast report being swamped with callers wanting to congratulate the new American hero. "They won't let it go. There's an intense frustration out there, and it bothers me," says Clark Weber of Chicago station WIND, one of the few to express concern over the intensity of the response and the unquestioning public support.

Across the nation, the letters to the editor are heavily in his favor, some newspapers reporting that, in the days and weeks immediately following the shootings, they received no letters of opposition at all. Cartoons appear to reflect the public mood. One depicts the entrance to the subway with a sign above it proclaiming: "Muggers 5000, Citizens 4." A figure labeled "Government" stands at the top of the stairwell shouting down into it: "Hey—you citizens knock off the rough stuff down there."

Los Angeles District Attorney Ira Reiner sees nothing wrong with this public response. "To live today in urban America means that you are severely at risk and essentially helpless to deal with the problem of crime. When someone comes along to make you feel you are not helpless, then everyone collectively throws their hats in the air."

But the response is not from urban America alone. From rural New England to hamlets in the West, where people still don't lock their cars on the street or the doors in their homes, comes news of excitement, words of support, expressions of rage about crime and criminals that surely are not born of personal experience.

The same feelings, the same fantasies, that have turned films like *Death Wish*, *Rambo* and *Dirty Harry* into smash hits, that have made national heroes of Charles Bronson, Sylvester Stallone and Clint Eastwood, are at work here. These movie stalwarts dazzle us with their audacity, thrill us with their daring, give legitimacy to our most violent fantasies. They assuage our anxieties about our own vulnerability, allow us to believe in justice again, leave us almost breathless with excitement and admiration.

Long before Bernie Goetz rocketed into our consciousness, we had made him up—made him up in the characters portrayed by Bronson, Eastwood and Stallone who enact for us the orgy of retribution we cannot permit ourselves. Charles Bronson sits on the subway with a bag of groceries, just like any ordinary guy carrying home his supper, and waits for some thug to come along and try it. Clint Eastwood points a gun at a man's head and taunts, "Go ahead, make my day." Bernie Goetz walks into a subway car and sits down in the middle of four black youths. Life and art stand in a reciprocal relationship to each other.

13· In the decade between 1950 and 1960, the Goetz family
continued to prosper, the elder Goetz becoming an increasingly
important real estate owner and businessman in Rhinebeck. It
was during this period that Bernhard Goetz decided to move his
New York factory to the foot of Wynkoop Lane—a plan that
soon embroiled him in controversy with his neighbors.

To Goetz, it wasn't just the convenience of having his business close at hand. He saw it also as providing jobs in a community where there were few. But most of the townspeople
were outraged, none more so than his neighbors on Wynkoop
Lane. The idea that there would be a factory on the corner of
their lovely country road left the neighborhood aghast. "We
couldn't understand how he could even think of doing something like that—a factory on a street like this," recalls a woman.

As the neighbors now tell it, Mr. Goetz listened politely, if
impatiently, as they came to explain their concerns for the neighborhood and to ask him to abandon the plan. But he stubbornly
insisted on his own way. He owned the property, he seemed to
them to be saying, bought it with his own sweat and blood, and
no one was going to tell him what he could do with it. "No matter
what anybody said, you couldn't move him," one man says, the

anger still plainly visible as he remembers the events of so long ago.

Word of their failure to penetrate Goetz's resolve passed from one household to another, and the neighbors began to meet, first in twos and threes, then in a larger group, hoping that their unified pressure would change his mind. But neither their efforts at persuasion nor their appeals to the Village Council were of any use. "People were furious. It wasn't only the people on this street either; it was the whole town," reports another neighbor. "He wasn't very well liked before, but after that I don't think anybody ever talked to him again." And pointing to the building abandoned over twenty years ago, he almost shouts, "And now we have to live with that damn eyesore."

The factory, the legacy of the Goetz family to their old neighbors, is indeed an ugly blemish on the landscape—the dilapidated structure rotting and rusting from disuse, some of the windows broken, some boarded up. The pavement in the parking lot has crumbled from years of neglect, and the metal fence surrounding it dips and weaves crazily as it continues to sink into a foundation that will no longer support its weight.

As neighborly relations with Mr. Goetz broke down, the impact was felt throughout the family. Although Gertrude Goetz wasn't seen as a very social person among her neighbors, until this time she had maintained cordial and helpful relations with them. Afterward they became almost completely estranged from her. No more friendly chats on the street as they exchanged gossip and recipes; no more visits when they compared notes about the children's growth and shared advice about this problem or that one.

They felt sorry for her, some of the old neighbors now say. But they were also deeply resentful. "It wasn't our fault that it came to that," remembers a woman. "It was his. I know it wasn't her fault either. Mrs. Goetz was really quite a nice person, kind of quiet, but nice. I guess she had to stick by her husband, or maybe he was the kind of man who did what he wanted, no matter who got hurt. I don't know. But people wouldn't have anything much to do with any of them after that."

The children, too, saw formerly friendly faces suddenly turned away. Until this time, the neighbors had been an amiable presence in their lives, sometimes offering a treat, almost always smiling warmly as they passed. After the conflict with their father, no one seemed to know how to behave. "Nobody wanted to punish the children for the father's sins," explains a woman, "but everybody was so uncomfortable about what happened— the kids, too—that you just sort of looked the other way when they were around. I think people must've felt they didn't know how to act to each other anymore."

For Bernie, about nine at the time, it would have been hard to grasp what had happened—to understand why people were so angry over the factory his father was building, why his father would have to do it when there was so much opposition. But since his father's decisions were unquestioned in the family, there was no one to ask. It would have been hard also for a child so young to confront the realization that his father wasn't re-spected outside the family. It could only have seemed incon-gruous, given the senior Bernhard's power and authority inside the house.

In such a situation, any child will likely be torn between anger at the offending parent and denial that the parental ideal could be tarnished. No matter which side of the ambivalence the child might come down on, there would be little comfort. To see his father as flawed would leave a child like Bernie frightened and vulnerable. To acknowledge his anger would mean he'd have to suffer his guilt and, with this particular father, even more fear than he already knew.

The isolation in the neighborhood would have been especially difficult for Bernie, matching and reinforcing as it did the ex-periences that were, by then, so commonplace at school. Yet he had no real choice. To see hostility in a neighbor's eyes would threaten to evoke his own anger at his father for putting him in this position. To warm to a smile would feel like a betrayal of the family covenant. Family members, after all, are supposed to be close, to stick together, to take each other's side. A child doesn't know why it has to be that way. It's like the law; it just is, that's all.

No surprise, then, that Bernie began to watch his feet as he walked by, afraid to look up and see a smile, afraid also that he wouldn't. "I felt sorry for the children, especially Bernie. He was always kind of a loner, but after people got mad because his father was building that factory, it seemed like he couldn't look right at you anymore," recalls a neighbor.

As he approached puberty, Bernie was a thin, wiry child, a lock of blond hair usually dangling perilously near his left eye, his glasses riding low on the bridge of his nose. He was a studious boy, one of the brightest kids in his class at the Rhinebeck Central School, interested in books, not sports; curious about the physical world, not people; wanting to know how things work— what causes sunspots, how electric currents flow from one place to another.

He managed his tears better than when he was smaller, apparently having learned to seal the pain on the inside so he could keep it from showing on the outside. But he still didn't seem to fit anywhere—not in school, not in the neighborhood. Even in the family, his quiet bookish ways, his quick clipped speech, his hunched hurried walk, all his nervous mannerisms, set him apart from the others.

By then he had developed the walk that still characterizes him now—a long-striding, rapid pace that defies anyone to keep up with him, his eyes downcast, his shoulders tight and high as if girding himself against the cold. To this day, he usually goes by so quickly that he seems like a blur, making it hard for anyone to see his sensitive face with its rather attractive features. When he was a boy, it must have been one way to get out of the schoolyard quickly, before the teasing started. It's as if he thought that if he looked busy, had someplace to go and something to do, his isolation wouldn't be so noticeable—not to them, not even to himself.

As is so often the case with lonely children, Bernie learned to keep himself company. On the surface at least, it didn't seem to matter so much if the other kids wouldn't play with him. No doubt in part as his defense against the pain of their rejection, the message they got is that he didn't think they were very smart or interesting anyway. "It's funny, but I always had this idea about Bernie that maybe he really thought he was better than the rest of us," remarks a former classmate. "Y'know, like he didn't care that much if the other kids thought he was a queer duck."

He didn't really seem to care either if there was no one around to talk to. It was as if it was more comfortable to converse with himself, safer and more predictable. "Nobody talked to him much, but sometimes if you did try to have a conversation with him, you'd get the crazy idea that you'd just interrupted him in the middle of something, I mean some kind of conversation that was going on in his head."

At home, too, he would spend most of his time alone, wandering in the woods behind the house when he wasn't bent over a book or trying to fix some piece of electrical equipment. His brother George recalls that he was a very "quiet kid [who was] not interested in sports and had only one hobby—collecting old electrical equipment."

When Bernie was ten years old, he suddenly acquired a roommate—Octavio Ramos, who at seventeen was brought into the family by the elder Goetz. They had met in Havana. Mr. Goetz was on vacation; Octavio was seeking to flee the pre-revolutionary Batista regime. Goetz invited him first to be a tour guide, then to share a swim and a walk, and, finally, to join the family in Rhinebeck.

With no advance warning, this young Cuban was moved into Bernie's neat, spartan bedroom, which they shared for the next two years. According to Octavio, Bernie was a very disciplined child, rising at the first signal of the alarm without further prompting, going to bed at his scheduled hour without any fuss. Already he showed evidence of the compulsion for order and neatness that would characterize both his adult personality and his personal environment. The room they shared, says Octavio, didn't look like a child's room—no toys, no childhood bric-a-brac anywhere in sight.

To Octavio, the elder Goetz became like a father, but a benevolent father, not the tyrannical one his own sons knew so well. He spoke to Octavio respectfully, treated him warmly, and set out to make a place for him in the business as if he were the heir apparent. Meanwhile, his own son George, the same age as Octavio, was ignored or, worse yet, treated contemptuously.

Despite Octavio's favored status, Bernie apparently felt close to him, turning to him for the companionship he found nowhere else. And Octavio speaks of young Bernie as a warm, loving boy —not a description heard often of Bernie Goetz at any age.

Did the family worry about their youngest member and his odd and lonely ways? No one is willing to say much about such matters, preferring to keep silent for fear of being misconstrued. But we know enough both about the patterns of family life in general and about this family in particular to assume that there was some concern at least. Almost certainly it would have been hard for a mother as conscientious as Gertrude Goetz not to worry about a child who seemed so isolated, so without a friend, hard for her not to wonder why this child would be so different from the others.

But very soon the whole family had something else, something much larger, to worry about. Less than three months after Bernie's twelfth birthday, his father was arrested, charged with sexually molesting two fifteen-year-old boys.

It was a stunning shock to the community, a nightmare for the family. It seemed impossible, the conspiracy of a couple of malcontents who, for reasons unknown, were angry at the elder Goetz. Everyone in town knew that, over the years, Mr. Goetz had hired teenagers to work in the factory weekends and summers. Did these boys work for him? Is that how they knew him? Were they dissatisfied with their wages, with the working conditions in the factory?

The pastoral village, looking so serene under its white winter blanket, was buzzing, the bitterness of an icy winter that had gone on too long forgotten in the presence of this hot news. "Have you heard . . . ?" women asked each other as they selected meat at the butcher's, groceries at the market. "Have you heard . . . ?" men asked each other when they met in the street, at lunch in the diner, or transacted their business over the telephone. Although he wasn't an admired member of the community, he was an important and powerful one. It was hard to believe he could be involved in anything so sordid. Yet why would these kids lie?

In some ways, the boys who accused Bernhard Goetz were the 1950s rural analog of the 1980s urban bad kids who tangled with his son almost exactly a quarter of a century later. Their reputations were unsavory—kids who were known to get into trouble and to be troublesome. One had been expelled from school, the other dropped out. By fifteen, they were pretty much on their own, uncontrolled by family rules or the social constraints of their time and place. Were they trying to shake Mr. Goetz down? Or could they have been telling the truth?

In hushed consternation, people reminded each other that, over the years, there had been rumors about Mr. Goetz and some other young boys. But no one had wanted to believe them. Not in a town like this; not someone you saw all the time, someone who looked and acted just like everyone else.

The family's public stance was a flat denial. But inside the house, away from prying eyes and ears, there was turmoil. Gertrude's passivity finally fell away as she flew into a rage on hearing the news and swept some of her best crystal and china crashing to the floor. Barbara and George were old enough to understand what had happened. But how could children of any age integrate the meaning of such an event? Surely their senses would have refused to take in this astonishing news. Their father, sexually molesting two young boys? It couldn't be. But if it wasn't true, then why these charges?

The younger children, Bernice and Bernie, could only have been frightened and bewildered. Even all these years later, Bernice says poignantly, "I didn't know what was going on at the time. I was a *child*." Yet there are no secrets in families, as experts in family relations tell us all the time, especially when it's something of this magnitude. At any age, when knowing is too threatening to the foundations of our security, we may not *want* to know what we can plainly see. So, as with adults who resist knowing what they know, children, too, will lock painful knowledge away somewhere inside and keep it outside conscious awareness. But any child, even a five-year-old, will notice that parents spend more time than usual talking behind closed doors, that the house seems filled with urgent whispers, that each time they walk into a room, the talk suddenly stops.

In the Goetz family, the younger children were twelve and fourteen. Even if the local newspaper suddenly disappeared from the front doorstep, they went to school; they saw a headline as they passed a newsstand; they heard talk. Inside the house, too, they surely would catch snatches of conversation, no matter how hidden; would notice the frightened look on the faces of the other members of the family; would feel the tensions that, in such a period of strain, communicate themselves in numberless unspoken ways.

When reasonable explanations aren't forthcoming, children of any age will learn to hold their tongues, to keep their questions to themselves, to try to deny the evidence of their senses. Bernie and Bernice undoubtedly did no less. But their silence and their efforts at denial would not be an indication that their fears had been allayed. Quite the contrary. Instead, their anxiety would only be heightened as they would wait and wonder and worry, all the while feeling scared and helpless, as if they were perched on the edge of a volcano from which there was no escape.

14· Nine-thirty Saturday evening, the end of a long day. Shirley Cabey, now thirty-nine years old, looks around her spotless kitchen wearily yet with satisfaction. "It looks nice," she thinks to herself. It's hard to keep it looking that way—the place so small, the walls and ceilings peeling no matter what she does, the kids always making such a mess. But it's worth the effort, makes her feel good to see everything in place.

She walks into the living room, flips on the TV and sits down for a few minutes of rest before tending to her seven-year-old daughter's bedtime routines.* The deliberately heated voice of a newscaster fills the small room: "Coming up at ten: Four youths shot on a subway in Manhattan this afternoon. Stay tuned for details."

"Wonder what happened," she thinks to herself absently as she gathers together wrapping paper and boxes. "Have to get on these Christmas presents as soon as I get her to bed. C'mon, honey, bedtime. Wash your hands and face good now; brush your teeth; no, not that way; here, let me show you again; there, that's better; under the covers now and mama'll read to you;

---

* This child was born four years after Ronald Cabey's death, the offspring of a primary relationship with a man who is still in Mrs. Cabey's life.

that's enough for tonight; we'll read more tomorrow; kiss mama good night now; good, that's my girl; sleep tight."

Back in the living room, she has missed the top story of the night, the shooting in the subway. "Well, what's the difference? Every day it's something, isn't it? Shooting, killing, people hurting each other. Seems like a terrible world these days."

A knock on the door interrupts her thoughts. Startled, she glances at the clock—10:10. She's a private person, doesn't have much to do with neighbors, has no friends in the building. "Wonder who that could be this time of night." She peers through the peephole and sees a woman who lives downstairs. Their last names are somewhat alike, so their mail gets mixed up sometimes. Since Mrs. Cabey's telephone isn't listed, this neighbor also occasionally gets telephone calls meant for someone in the Cabey family.

Even before Mrs. Cabey gets the door unbolted, her neighbor, trying unsuccessfully to keep her voice calm, is saying, "I just got a phone call from the transit police. They thought my boy was shot this afternoon, but he's home right now, so I told them it couldn't be him and maybe they got the names mixed up. They said you should call; here's the number."

"Thanks," says Mrs. Cabey, trying to still her trembling as she reaches for the piece of paper the woman holds in her extended hand.

"Are all your boys home?" the other woman inquires.

"No, no, they're not all here, just two," she replies, her voice trailing off as her mind scurries about trying to think where those who are missing might be. "Darrell's at my mother's, taking care of her," she explains, more in an effort to reassure herself than to continue this conversation. "Well, I better call; thanks again."

She stands quietly for a moment, her head leaning against the door, drained of all feeling except the fatigue which now settles itself down in her bones. "Oh God, don't let it be." Rousing herself, she goes to the phone on the wall above the couch in the living room, dials the number she holds in her hand and, already knowing what she'll hear, waits for a voice to answer. "This is Shirley Cabey. Someone called and said my son Darrell has been shot."

She mobilizes herself quickly, the tiredness gone now. She calls her mother, who has just prepared herself for bed. "Darrell's been shot; he's in the hospital, St. Vincent's, all the way downtown someplace." Neither woman knows exactly where it is. But her mother responds immediately; she'll dress at once and be ready in fifteen, twenty minutes.

That done, Mrs. Cabey turns her attention to the next problem. How will they get to the hospital at this hour? She phones a cousin who lives nearby and has a car. Don't worry, the cousin assures her; she'll come quickly. "Will you stop and pick up mama, too?" Mrs. Cabey asks. "Of course," her cousin replies. Shirley Cabey now has nothing to do but sit and wait.

In a few minutes, she calms down a bit. In her world, shootings, violence of all kinds, are common, part of the experience of everyday life. It makes her angry to think about the brutality in this neighborhood, about how much blood is spilled needlessly and heedlessly. And it frightens her as well. But when you see as many people hurt by violence as she has in her years in the project, you also come to some uneasy acceptance of it as part of the daily ration.

So as she waits, she tries to soothe herself. "It's probably no big thing," she tells herself. "People get shot all the time; somebody's always getting shot or something around here," she reminds herself as she runs through in her mind all the shootings that have touched her awareness recently. "Then next thing you know, they're right back out on the street," she concludes, heartened by the thought.

Still, it seems like a long time before a knock on the door signals the arrival of her mother and cousin. She gathers up her things and the three move quickly, hoping to catch the elevator before it glides off to answer another call.

Once in the car, she begins to fret and worry again. "Maybe it's just a finger or something," she says hopefully.

Her mother, who worked as a nurse's aide in Bronx Hospital for twenty-six years before her retirement three years ago, assumes an outward certainty she doesn't feel. "It can't be nothing too serious; otherwise they would've called before this time of night."

It's a long way from the Bronx down to Greenwich Village, where St. Vincent's Hospital is located. But there's not much traffic out, so the ride goes quickly. Shortly before midnight, the three women walk hesitantly through the hospital's corridors looking for someone to talk to. Everything's quiet this time of night, even in a hospital as big as this one. Finally they find the Admitting Office and in it a sleepy clerk. "No," he insists with a yawn, "we don't have no Darrell Cabey listed."

Mrs. Cabey perseveres. "The transit police told me my son was shot and he's here."

"Oh, that one. Why didn't you say so? 'Course, I don't have him; he ain't been admitted yet. Why don't you go down to Emergency. They probably got something on him down there."

The women stand before him uncertainly, not knowing where to go. Pointing the direction, he says impatiently, "Through that doorway, turn right and go back the way you came. When you get outside, turn left, go up to the corner, then take another left. You can't miss it; it's got a big sign that says 'Emergency Entrance.' "

"I'm Shirley Cabey; the police called and told me my son Darrell was shot and he's here," she repeats to the clerk in the Emergency Room.

"Oh yes, Mrs. Cabey. He's still in surgery. Why don't you sit down; a doctor will come and talk to you as soon as they're finished."

They sit, but now her mind goes blank, the words "still in surgery" reverberating there and pushing everything else out. Her mother and cousin are talking to her, trying to sound normal, but she can't make sense of anything they're saying. All she can hear are the words "still in surgery."

The wait seems endless. How long is it? Ten minutes! It's like an eternity. Half hour! What could be wrong? Forty-five minutes! An hour! What's taking so long?

Each lost in her own thoughts, the three women sit silently now, eyes downcast—waiting, worrying. Mrs. Cabey looks up to see a man in surgical greens approaching, his face set in sad, serious lines. "God, don't let him be dead." She struggles to her feet as the doctor comes to a halt before her. Shaking his head sadly, he says, "I'm sorry, Mrs. Cabey; there was nothing we could do. The bullet severed his spinal cord; Darrell will be paralyzed from the waist down; he'll never walk again."

Paralyzed! Never walk again! Not just a small wound! The unimaginable has finally happened. No, it's not true, can't be true. It was supposed to be just a little hole, maybe in a finger or a hand. "Where is he? I want to see my boy." No, the doctor says, she can't see Darrell now; he's in Recovery.

"Does he know?" No, he's not conscious yet, so they couldn't tell him; maybe it's best if she does that tomorrow. He'll be awake then, better able to understand. For now, it's best to go home and get some rest, he advises kindly. Darrell will need her strength tomorrow.

But she can't leave, not yet. Here in the hospital she feels closer to her son; the Bronx is so far away. So she sits down again, numbly repeating the doctor's words over and over in her head. Paralyzed. Never walk again. She heard him say it, but her mind resists. This is the tragedy she has feared yet never believed would happen—not to her, not to one of her children, not to Darrell, dear God, not to Darrell.

At last her mother and cousin persuade her to come home. One on each side, they lead her out, following the same corridors through which they came a couple of hours ago. Anxiously, they keep glancing at her as she moves heavily between them, their eyes meeting in silent acknowledgment of their helplessness.

They're back in her apartment in the Bronx; her mother offers to stay the night. No, she'll be all right, she assures her. She needs to be alone, to think, to come to terms with this terrible night. After they leave, she sits in her living room surrounded by gift boxes and Christmas wrapping. Bitter tears scald her eyes, her cheeks. Why? Why?

Wearily she pulls herself up, walks to her bedroom, undresses and lies down on her bed. But there'll be no sleep tonight. She tosses and turns fitfully, reviewing her life, her concern for Darrell over these last months. Guiltily, she asks herself, "Did I do something wrong? What could I have done different?" Anguished, she replies, "I tried everything I know. I prayed, and I tried to talk to him; Lord, you know how I tried."

She knows life hasn't been easy for any of them, not for her, not for the children. But until now she didn't think she had much to complain about. She'd always made do. Sometimes when she looked around her, she even thought they were luckier than most. But she also knew it had been a long time since any-one in the family had had any extras.

Still, it had been getting better recently. With the children growing up, she was able to think about getting a job, something where she'd earn some money and make life a little easier for all of them. She was lucky; she hadn't even looked very long when she found a job as a food service worker in a mental hospital. It's hard work, but she doesn't mind. She likes getting out of the

96 /

house every day almost as much as she appreciates the money. "It's nice to work because then you have something interesting to talk about when you see your friends," she says as she talks about her job.

Her probationary period ended just two weeks ago, on December 8. She was proud when they told her she was a good worker and her job was permanent. What would happen now? She hated to give it up when she just really got started. But would they let her take some time off to take care of Darrell? "Oh Lord, why?"

Toward morning, she dozes a bit, then wakes with a start. Is someone in the room? She sits up, looks around and shakes herself fully awake. "What's the matter with you? You going crazy or something?" But the feeling persists.

She knows she has to pull herself together, so she tries to shake it off. She has to tell the other children about their brother. Those who were home last night know he's been shot, but they don't know yet how bad it is. They'll be upset. But she won't really have time to tend to any of them. She has to get to the hospital; Darrell will need her today.

What can she tell them? She still doesn't know what happened, only that Darrell and three boys she never heard of were shot on the subway. No one knows who did it or why. It all sounds so crazy to her, so unreal. How can she make sense of it for them?

She gets up, dresses, wakes the children, tells them the news. As they recover from the shock, they ply her with questions. "I don't know," she keeps repeating. "Maybe we'll know more later today. Right now, I need you all to be good because I got to go to the hospital."

Early Sunday morning, Shirley Cabey boards the subway, sits down on the nearly empty bench and gives her body over to the rocking and swaying of the train. She's still thinking about the experience of the morning when it seemed that someone was talking to her. She feels oddly comforted by her thoughts, as if something positive is on the horizon, if only she can grab hold of it. She's even a little less frightened of having to tell Darrell that he'll never walk again. Still, she shudders as the words come to mind. How will he react? What will become of him?

As her mind jumps uneasily from one set of thoughts to another, she watches nervously for the station coming up. She doesn't ride the subway into Manhattan often, certainly not this far downtown. Now the signs tell her that the train is approaching Fourteenth Street, her station, the same one from which the gunman boarded the train the day before. She gathers herself together, rises to her feet, steadies herself against a post and waits for the train to grind to a halt.

It's unseasonably mild on this Sunday before Christmas, and the winter sun warms her as she walks toward the hospital. Suddenly she stops in her tracks, feeling once again that some strange force is reaching out to her. She recognizes the feeling as a familiar one, yet can't quite place it.

She walks another half block, then stops again, overcome. She understands now; God has been trying to send her a message. "Lord, Lord, I hear you. My Darrell's been drifting toward trouble, and I've been praying for him, asking you to help him. This must be your way of looking after him. Maybe it's not just a tragedy; maybe you knew what you were doing, Lord. There's a lot you can do from a wheelchair if you learn how to use your head. He can't go out on the streets no more, so now he can go back to school and finish his education. Maybe he'll even go to college. Thank you, God, for answering my prayers."

With her head held higher and her step firmer, she walks into the hospital. Her own faith restored, she knows now that she can help her son. Resolutely she walks up to the desk and asks for his room. "Your son's in Intensive Care, Mrs. Cabey. You can go on up and see him, but just for a few minutes. We only allow visitors for ten minutes an hour in Intensive Care."

Her heart clutches. "Intensive Care! It sounds so awful." The words thrust upon her anew the reality of his condition. Could it be that his life actually is in danger? "Dear, sweet Lord, please, let him live."

Her steps now slowed, she tries to banish the terrible thoughts that crowd in on her as she finds the elevator and goes up to the floor where Darrell lies. She walks toward the heavy doors separating the Intensive Care Unit from the rest of the floor, pulls one of the doors open, steps into the room, and shrinks at the vision before her. So many beds; so many people with tubes sticking out of them; so many nurses rushing to and fro, their rubber soles making small squeals and odd whooshing sounds as they cross the floor. She stands in the doorway uncertainly, timidly, trying to regain her composure. A nurse sees her. "Can I help you?" she asks in a voice just above a whisper.

"I've come to see my son, Darrell Cabey."

"Certainly, Mrs. Cabey"—her finger pointing down the row of beds. "He's right down there, the fourth bed."

With a shudder, she walks down the aisle trying not to look at the beds she passes. No one should be seen like this—no dignity, no privacy, no way to protect yourself from prying eyes. "The fourth bed; here it is." Now she can look. Her breath catches in her throat at what she sees—tubes in his nose, in his arms, wires from all those machines connected to somewhere on his body.

He seems so small, fragile, not like her nineteen-year-old son, her young man. She tiptoes around to the side of the bed and stands there, looking down on him wordlessly. She wants to reach out and gather him into her arms as she used to do when he was a small child. But she hardly dares to touch him for fear of disturbing the tubes and wires.

Is he asleep? He seems scarcely to be breathing. His eyelids quiver, as if struggling against a great weight; then slowly they open. He looks in her direction, has trouble focusing for a few seconds, finally recognizes her. Weakly, his fingers flutter, trying to reach out to her, tears streaming uncontrolled from his eyes. Nearly overwhelmed with her own pain, she grasps his hand and bends down to hear the words his lips are trying to form. "I'm sorry, mama; I'm so sorry."

In a few minutes, the nurse comes to say her time is up. "I'll be back, son, y'hear? I'll be back soon. You get some rest now." She isn't sure he hears her; he seems to have slipped away again.

Outside, she goes into the waiting room with others like herself, people with loved ones in Intensive Care who wait for the next ten-minute visit. Two men and a woman are playing cards. Two women are talking, making conversation to distract themselves. A few people sit with magazines or books, some turning pages idly, others having already given up the pretense of reading. The television set is on but the few who try to watch are easily distracted. Before she can find a place to sit, a doctor appears in the doorway. "Mrs. Cabey, I'd like to talk with you."

Fighting down a sense of foreboding, she walks with him into the corridor, where he stops a few feet from the waiting-room door. For the first time, she hears that her son is even more gravely ill than she had realized. The bullet that severed Darrell's spine also pierced his lungs. She can't grasp it. "What does it mean?" They can't say yet; it's too early to know. There's a danger of pneumonia, a very real danger, and if that happens, well, there's no predicting. He doesn't mean to frighten her, but she must know the facts. Darrell's not in shape to fight off a major infection.

By evening, Darrell is more alert. Even though his brain is still benumbed from the anesthetic and the opiates they've been giving him since he came out of surgery, they can talk a bit. The question she's been dreading finally comes. "Am I gonna to be all right, mama?"

She's been rehearsing her answer all day, yet now she can hardly get the words out. She hesitates, then drawing in her breath, she takes his hand in both of hers and explains his situation to him. He listens, seeming to take the news quietly, his eyes never leaving her face. When she finishes speaking, he stares up at the ceiling mutely. He has no words, only tears.

In the days that follow, Shirley Cabey watches and waits as her son fights to stave off the pneumonia that threatens his damaged lungs. But the infection takes hold, and the real battle for his life is joined. For eighteen days, she prays and he fights. Then, on January 9, he stops breathing.

"Code Blue, Code Blue," a disembodied voice commands urgently over the speaker system. The emergency staff rushes to Darrell's bed, working quickly and heroically to bring life back into his frail body. They succeed, but not soon enough. Darrell Cabey, now kept alive by a respirator, has slipped into a coma. If he lives, the doctors tell his mother, he'll be brain-damaged.

15· Throughout the month of January, the Goetz lore grows. A waitress in a New Jersey diner where he stops to eat says, "I almost dropped my tray when he walked in. I got one of our postcards and he wrote something on it and signed his name." When asked what he wrote, she replies quite seriously, "I still haven't figured out what it means. He wrote my name, 'To Irene,' then it says, 'To be trusted is a better compliment than to be loved.' But it doesn't matter; it's something to hold on to for the future."

As press and public grasp eagerly for any word about this man who has catapulted into public consciousness so unexpectedly, hundreds of reporters, now not just from New York but from all over the world, stand guard at his Fourteenth Street apartment building, waiting for they know not what. Still insisting that he wants no publicity, Bernie grants an exclusive interview with the New York *Post* two days after his release from jail. Munching on a chicken sandwich and sipping coffee in a neighborhood restaurant where he has long been a customer and is now a cherished luminary, he tells the reporter, "I'm amazed at this celebrity status. I want to remain anonymous." No one thinks to ask how he expects to remain anonymous while talking to the press.

. . .

Everyone in the neighborhood, whether they live there or just work there, has been touched by the events of December 22. The people who work in this coffee shop are no exception. From early morning until late into the night, they have been deluged by the press, hammered at and badgered by reporters for any tidbit they might be able to supply.

How often does he come in? What does he eat for lunch? For dinner? Is he a generous tipper? When did you last see him? What did he say? Just good morning, nothing more? Surely there's something else you can remember. What was he wearing? Does he always eat alone? Does he have a girlfriend? Have you ever seen him with a woman? With a man? With anyone?

Some people are fed up with it by now. There are murmurings among some of Bernie's neighbors, grumblings about the chaos he's brought into their lives. They're tired of the crowds outside, tired of having to fight their way into their own home, tired of the cameras and the people, of the constant invasion of their privacy.

Others, like most of the workers in the coffee shop, are enthralled by all the excitement, feeling alive and important for the first time in years, sometimes for the first time ever. Who paid attention to them before? Who cared what they thought?

Since Bernie's life and theirs have come together in this unexpected way, they now have a proprietary interest in him— in who he is, what he does, how he lives, even whom he talks to. When he comes into the restaurant, therefore, they hover near, watching over him protectively, keeping a path around his table clear. In this way, they shield him from intrusion while also preserving their own sense of pride in ownership. It's they who get to steer away from his table people they decide are idle curiosity seekers, they who bring to him those they know and want to impress.

For Bernie, who has been a customer in this coffee shop for

all the years he has lived on Fourteenth Street, his new role there represents a dramatic change from the past. Until now, he came and went almost unnoticed, just another customer, albeit an odd one. "He was one of those quiet types, polite and all that, but didn't look straight at you and didn't talk hardly at all," says one of the staff. It's a friendly place, so from time to time people made overtures. But it was obvious that he couldn't think what to say or how to say it. Generally, therefore, he was left alone to eat his simple meals in silence.

Now here, as elsewhere, he's more likely to respond when others speak to him, even initiates conversation himself at times. He's still awkward at it, still speaks in a disconnected, speedy style that's hard to follow. But he does speak to them now, and he's listened to attentively, even if not always understood. "He's a funny one," says another staff member. "Used to be you couldn't get hardly a word out of him. Now it's like he enjoys talking, like he got to be friendlier since . . . ," his words trailing off as if he were about to say something embarrassing. "But, y'know, it's hard to figure what he's saying, like he talks in riddles a lot of times."

As public and media are joined together in glorifying Bernie Goetz, Les Payne, a black man who is also the national editor of *Newsday*, watches and listens. "Goetz disappeared into the subway tunnel a fleeing gunman," he writes, "and emerged a fugitive darling of the law-abiding public. . . . What would have been the public reaction if, instead of what police described as a 'golden blond,' a black passenger, say, on the Harlem D train had pulled an unlicensed pistol and shot four black teenagers under the same circumstances? . . . What if the gunman had been black and his victims four white teenagers? . . . In neither hypothetical case would there have been the frenzied lust for blood and the accompanying embrace, nay worship, of the subway gunman. . . . [But] the world knows that black teenagers are subway muggers. In picking up the gun, Goetz, the blond hero, struck a blow for white manhood."

Two weeks later, as if to confirm what Payne had written, New York *Times* columnist Sydney Schanberg gives the world a view of his mailbag in which one letter announces exuberantly: "Bernhard Hugo Goetz makes me proud, P-R-O-U-D, to be a white, male American! At long last we can hold up our heads again!" And a graffito on the wall of the subway station at Fourteenth Street and Sixth Avenue, the one Bernie Goetz uses all the time, proclaims proudly: "Goetz Rules Niggers."

Slowly the word "racism" enters the public dialogue. Some of the same people who are now applauding Bernie Goetz marched in Selma, Alabama, just twenty years ago. What happened in those intervening years? some people begin to ask. Harvard professor James Q. Wilson says, "There are no more liberals on the crime and law-and-order issue in New York because they've all been mugged. . . . The normal partisan divisions no longer obtain in a situation of this sort." But long before anyone knew what sort of situation this was, minds were made up.

Meanwhile, as small victories are being celebrated and messages of joy and congratulations are directed to Goetz, the boys who were shot and their families are hearing different words—letters that contain filthy, racist slurs; that tell Shirley Cabey, Darrell's mother, that it's too bad her son has *only* been paralyzed, that express regret that the others will walk again, that threaten to do them violence of one kind or another.

"All you slimey Niggers should get it between the eyes."

"We should exterminate you lousey Roaches."

"I'll recognize you when you get out of the hospital, nigger watch your black ass."

"You fucking, mother fucking nigger, I hope you suffer the torments of hell."

"Daryl's black ass is finished. I'm so sorry it's not your son too."

"Too bad your slezzbag son isn't dead."

"Black mama, just know, some day, some way I'm going to kill your stinking nigger son."

"Too bad that man only paralyzed Darrel. He should be dead DEAD."

"It's too bad you're not a helpless cripple too. Maybe next time."

"From now on, watch out nigger."

No one talks much about these letters and the terrible hate and rage they express. It's not hot news. Instead, most reporters and observers still deny there's any racism involved in the public response, insisting it's nothing more than a human response to a criminal justice system that has failed in its job of protecting the innocent from the guilty. And people all over start a conversation about the case with "I'm not a racist, but . . ."

As everyone waits eagerly for the results of the grand jury investigation, new stories appear daily. Within a week after he's freed on bail, Bernie Goetz and Frank Brenner find themselves with, as Brenner puts it, "a basic, irreconcilable disagreement" over a strategy for the defense. Court experts guess that Goetz refused Brenner's advice either to try to cut a deal on a lesser charge or to go for some form of an insanity defense. But neither Bernie nor Brenner will comment.

On January 15, headlines announce that Bernie has hired new lawyers, Joseph Kelner and Barry Slotnick, two well-known attorneys, who will represent him in both the criminal case and the civil suits that are sure to follow. The man who two weeks ago wanted no legal representation now has two of the most high-powered attorneys in the city of New York in his employ.

The speculations of the courtroom pundits about the rift

between Goetz and Brenner are given substance by Slotnick's statement that his client wants to win "on the facts and not on a legal technicality." No matter what the charges, there will be no guilty plea. Bernie Goetz acted in self-defense, the waiting world is told.

As the noise continues to escalate, the politicians jump into and out of the fray. At a hearing of the Congressional Crime Caucus in Washington, New York Senator Alfonse D'Amato speaks in Goetz's defense, saying that the subways are so dangerous that riders need an armed guard. "I'm afraid to get in that subway system even when I'm with my bodyguard, and my bodyguard is afraid." A comment that prompts Mayor Koch to suggest acidly that he find a better bodyguard.

Joseph Kelner, one of Bernie's lawyers, has come to Washington to testify before the Caucus. On hearing D'Amato's remarks, he asks gleefully if the senator would be willing to serve as an expert witness about the hazards of riding the subways unprotected. Smiling when he hears D'Amato's affirmative reply, Kelner warns him that he might call him on behalf of the defense in the Goetz case. "You can," the senator tells him. "I've been on the subway when these young thugs come in there, and they don't even have to approach you," he declares. "They are menacing people by their very presence."

His anger at D'Amato notwithstanding, the mayor begins to count the political cost of the tough position he took when the shootings first occurred. He backs down. Maybe there's more to the story than he understood at first, he speculates aloud. "We don't know if he's a victim or a villain," he now says of Bernie. Maybe we should wait and see before making a judgment. After all, people have good reason for the fear they express. Let the grand jury decide if a crime has been committed.

. . .

With the entry of Kelner and Slotnick, the PR assault on the press and public begins in earnest. This is no longer just a case, albeit a sensational one. It is a cause. "We are proud and privileged to represent him in this great cause that affects the safety and welfare of all Americans, rich and poor, old and young, black and white," announces Kelner.

Very soon after they enter the case, Bernie's new lawyers notify Manhattan District Attorney Robert Morgenthau that Goetz is considering testifying before the grand jury. Calling a news conference in his office, Kelner makes the announcement to the press, insisting that Bernie has nothing to hide. He's not a vigilante, doesn't like being called that, he tells the assembled reporters. He's just a sweet, gentle, soft-spoken guy who normally wouldn't harm a fly. He, Kelner, can't even imagine him in a violent act. Bernie wants to tell his story, in fact, is eager to do so because he wants people to understand, wants to clear away any doubts about him as a hardworking, law-abiding citizen. "He is the personification of the finest we can produce in America."

Slotnick, too, has something to say. After repeating much of what Kelner has already said, he tells of his lengthy Sunday meeting with Bernie and how he is now convinced of his client's innocence. He was attacked on the subway and responded appropriately, Slotnick maintains. Now he hopes there "will be less fear and more safety because of him . . . that as a result of this unfortunate incident the citizenry and the officials of the city will realize just how vital it is to make our city and our subways safer. . . . He is a humanitarian. . . . I am sure he will be exonerated by a jury."

Meanwhile, in response to their questions, District Attorney Morgenthau tells the press he would be pleased to have Goetz testify before the grand jury. The decision on whether or not to indict will be delayed, he says, to give Goetz's attorneys "the opportunity to talk to us."

. . .

As they continue to make their position public, the shape of the defense strategy becomes visible. Bernhard Goetz, his lawyers tell us, acted "reasonably and understandably in a life-threatening situation, with money being demanded of him. He was surrounded in a four-on-one confrontation. He did not take the law into his own hands. He had the right to defend himself in these circumstances when there was no police present to protect him."

It's clear: self-defense will be the plea.

But the law on self-defense in New York State leaves wide latitude for interpretation. A person may use deadly force, the law says, if it is necessary to defend himself against the "imminent use of unlawful physical force" and if he *"reasonably believes"* that he is about to be hurt or killed, or about to become the victim of one of five other types of crime—rape, sodomy, robbery, kidnapping or burglary.

Before resorting to force, however, the intended victim must withdraw if able to do so safely. But even on this, the law is not cut-and-dried. For if a person *believes* he is in danger, the duty to retreat no longer holds.

What if a person is mistaken in judging the intentions of someone who seems to be threatening? He would still be entitled to use such physical force as he *reasonably believes* to be necessary to prevent a robbery, or any one of the other crimes covered by the statute, that he *reasonably believes* is about to happen.

The case against Bernie Goetz, then, will turn on what he might have *reasonably* believed. A difficult decision for the twenty-three men and women of the grand jury—six blacks, seventeen whites—New Yorkers all, who share his anger and his fear and who now must decide his fate.

16 · In the Goetz family, only Gertrude could not have been wholly surprised when her husband was arrested. She alone knew that he already had one conviction for giving alcoholic beverages to a minor—a misdemeanor for which he was fined a hundred dollars in 1958. In that case, he had picked up a hitchhiker, a boy from the *Herald Tribune*'s camp for underprivileged kids, took him to the factory, and kept him there late into the night while feeding him a dozen or so shots of cognac.

There was no talk that time of any molestation. But given the circumstances, it's hardly possible that the thought never crossed Mrs. Goetz's mind, especially when her husband seemed not to have learned his lesson. According to Octavio Ramos, Goetz often entertained teenage boys—sometimes at home, sometimes at the farm—and served them alcoholic drinks. If Octavio, who knew nothing of Goetz's earlier conviction, worried about the practice, it's unlikely that Gertrude would have done less.

Indeed, no matter how vigilant she might have been, even the best mechanisms of denial probably would have failed at times to keep her doubts and fears from forcing themselves upon her. Such doubts may be cut down, cast aside, ruthlessly shoved out of consciousness. Yet they return in moments when the controls are loosened—during the day when the mind unexpectedly roams free, at night in that brief period just before sleep fully overtakes consciousness. It's undoubtedly because of what she knew and what she feared that she became so enraged when her husband was caught and charged again, only this time with a much more serious crime than before, one they would not be able to keep quiet.

On February 23, 1960, Bernhard William Goetz was indicted on eighteen counts of "endangering the life and health of a child" and "assault in the 3rd degree"—charges brought against him by David Francis Mitchell and Austin James Fetzer, both fifteen years old. By then, the news had become so public that no one could be shielded from it any longer. For the children, whatever explanations their parents offered could have been no less perplexing, no less alarming, than the silence that went before.

Until this time, Bernie had been a protected child, brought up in an era when parents didn't deal easily with sex and sexuality, their own or their children's. Then, without warning, he had to deal with the news that his father stood accused of sexually molesting two boys not very much older than himself.

For any child, the emergence of adolescent sexual feelings can be frightening and, most of the time, are neither welcome nor comprehensible. They come so unexpectedly, as if from nowhere; they're so powerful. But even as they provoke anxiety, they also stimulate curiosity. This is the time when a child will lie in bed, at one moment resisting the temptations of the body these new feelings stir, at the next giving in to them. Explorations that leave the child with an odd mix of responses—the pleasurable sensations touch brings alternating with the uneasy sense of guilt and fear.

For Bernie, this period would have had to be complicated by the charges against his father. It's hard to imagine a situation more anguishing for a twelve-year-old boy and, at the same time, one more fraught with ambivalence—with titillation and fear, revulsion and attraction. How could he not have wondered what happened between his father and those boys, what it would feel like, what made his father do it? How could he not have felt shame? And anxiety? Small wonder his sister describes him at this time as seeming "very coiled up."

People who have observed Bernie for years testify that they've never seen him with a lover of either gender, that he seems to them to be a relatively asexual person. Certainly this is the image he presents to the world—a functional adaptation given the way his twelve-year-old mind must have connected his own nascent sexuality to his father's transgression. If an adult's sexual impulses could be so uncontrollable that they would jeopardize the whole family, how could the child believe he could master these feelings now welling up inside him with such unexpected intensity? One way certainly would be to maintain rigid control over his own fantasies and to punish himself harshly for any sign of a sexual wish, thought or feeling—a common response among children who have reason to fear their rising sexuality.

In muting his sexual self, he could accomplish another aim as well. If he couldn't find such feelings in himself, he could more easily maintain the denial of his father's guilt. If, after all, they didn't exist in him, he could believe they didn't exist in his father either. And maybe, just maybe, if he could gain that much control, he could make the whole nightmarish business disappear.

But it didn't go away. Nor were his parents able to protect him from the ugly publicity, rumors and gossip that flew around Rhinebeck and the surrounding communities. By the time February came to a close, Bernie was living in the middle of a maelstrom.

Barbara, the only one of the children who was out of the house by then, speaks of how difficult this period was on the others. And a neighbor remembers that "the family seemed to be in hiding," adding sympathetically, "It must have been awful."

Surely it must have been. How could any member of this family walk out the door comfortably, knowing what people in this small town were thinking even when they weren't talking?

Whatever the strains between Gertrude and Bernhard during this time, on one thing they stood together: The younger children could not be allowed to remain in the community. The prospect for continuing injury was too great. So they began to lay plans to send Bernie and his sister Bernice to a boarding school.

For Bernie, whose only real attachments were in the family, this was agonizing news, coloring the whole period with horror and disbelief. "Bernie was always very attached to both my parents," his sister Bernice recalls. Then, long before he was ready to leave them, they said he must go.

No amount of tears and pleading, no tantrums, no moody withdrawals, would move the parents. Their resolve was firm; the children must go. As the summer edged to a close, Bernie and his sister were sent as far away as their parents could get them— to a boarding school in Switzerland. For the family, a moment of sadness and pain; for a child, an abandonment that would not soon be forgotten.

At first glance, the decision to send the children away seems a sensible one. In similar circumstances, any of us might do the same if we could afford it. But if the children's welfare was so paramount in the minds and hearts of Gertrude and Bernhard Goetz, why were three of them—George, Bernice and twelve-year-old Bernie—brought to court to sit with their mother every day of the trial? There can be only one answer: Bernhard Goetz needed to present himself in the context of a family united by love and constancy, a family ready to brave the pain and humiliation of this sordid trial in order to make a public declaration of their faith in his innocence. Courtroom strategy was more important than the children's well-being.

To this day, the children insist upon their father's innocence, arguing that his personal and political enemies were out to get him, that the prosecutor had a political grudge to square, that David and Austin were not just a couple of nice kids who were victimized, but instead were trying to set their father up. Accusations that may be true but that have little to do with the charges against Bernhard Goetz.

The story the trial record tells is not a pretty one: David was the first to meet Mr. Goetz, a meeting that led to his accepting an invitation to spend an evening with him in an apartment adjacent to the family farmhouse. During that time, Goetz in the language of the complaint, "did place his hands in, upon and about the private parts" of David. At the end of this evening, Goetz offered David a job at the factory and, when he dropped him off at his house, held out to him a five-dollar bill.

Five dollars. Years later, another "bad kid," this one named Troy instead of David, asked Bernhard Goetz's son for five dollars. Was there some connection, even if an unconscious one, between Bernie's response to Troy and his knowledge of that earlier transaction between his father and David?

We know that the child at the trial heard David accuse his father of offering him five dollars. No matter what the public stance, it's impossible to conceive he could have listened to this and the other evidence against his father without encountering some internal doubt about his innocence. No matter how sturdy his mechanisms of denial, he could not have heard the boys' stories about his father's behavior without burning with shame.

Even if such painful knowledge had been wholly repressed for all the years between the trial and his meeting with Troy on the subway, it would not be completely gone. Rather it would lie inside him like a trap waiting to be sprung. Troy's request could certainly have been the trigger, tapping the buried memory of his father's accusers, of his own humiliation as he sat in the court-room and listened. The last straw for Bernie, the insult that finally stirred the rage inside him to the boiling point?

As the trial continues, the boys tell the court that not long after David's first evening with Mr. Goetz, he and his friend Austin went to the factory at around closing time and asked Goetz to take them out to the farm so that Austin could see it. They spent from seven o'clock to midnight together in the same apartment, during which time Goetz fondled both boys and exposed himself to them as well.

It's unclear why the boys allowed themselves to get involved with Mr. Goetz. Perhaps it was a lark for them, a way to torture an old man. Perhaps it was a way to satisfy their own sexual curiosity and interest while, at the same time, denying any responsibility for what happened. Perhaps they thought it was a good way to get Austin a job since it had worked for David. Perhaps they just wanted money. He had, after all, already offered David five dollars. Perhaps they did indeed plan to blackmail Mr. Goetz.

David swore that after their last meeting he called Goetz and asked him for ten dollars to pay a bill. Goetz's response, according to David, was to invite him to "come on up and get it." Yet when State Trooper Donoghue, the man who arrested Goetz, asked him if he thought the boys were trying to shake him down, he said no.

Bernhard Goetz did not testify in his own defense, but the testimony of others was damaging. Trooper Donoghue attested that Goetz, who was very worried about what would happen to him, had confessed his guilt at the time of the arrest and kept asking for his advice on what to tell and how to tell it. "He stated at that time that he let his emotions get away with him and that he went too far with the boys and that he had known he had done wrong," Donoghue told the court. "He admitted that he had rubbed their privates but that he had never taken them out of their pants, and at that time I also asked him about the Fetzer boy telling me that he had exposed himself when Mitchell wasn't there, and he admitted that was true and that was the only time that he had done it."

A Goetz employee, Katy Teator, called by the defense as a character witness, admitted under cross-examination that for some time it had been "rumored in the community that he likes young boys." Others corroborated her testimony.

After weighing the evidence, the trial court found Bernhard Goetz guilty on eight of the eighteen counts in the original indictment. The others were dismissed for technical reasons. Sentence: six months in jail. An appeal delayed the carrying out of the sentence.

In June 1963, the Court of Appeals dismissed four more counts on technicalities and ordered a new trial. By then, everyone had apparently had enough, and Goetz's attorneys engineered a plea bargain. He pleaded guilty to one charge of disorderly conduct: Sentence suspended.

The trial and the various appeals consumed the lives of Gertrude and Bernhard Goetz for almost three and a half years. Interestingly, during all this time, the elder Goetzes were sufficiently closemouthed about their ordeal so that Gertrude's sister, who was close enough to accompany her on her frequent visits to the children in Switzerland, knew nothing about the events of these years. Asked by a reporter recently about her brother-in-law's trial, she replied with astonishment, "What trial?"

By the time it was all over, the family as Bernie Goetz had known it was gone forever. Before his years in Switzerland were done, his parents had left Rhinebeck in shame. He would never go home again.

17· Just as the media have become part of the story, not simply the reporters of it, so have the attorneys for the principals in the case. Even before Bernie Goetz was identified, the well-known Manhattan criminal lawyer, Harry Lipsig, publicly announced that he would take the case without fee if the subway vigilante would come forward. After the arrest, others rushed to volunteer.

Some were already in the big leagues of their profession, well-established criminal lawyers who saw in Goetz yet another chance to increase their visibility and enhance their status. Others were young attorneys looking for their big break, the big case that would help them make their mark in the tough field of criminal law. "Sure, I would have loved to be part of the defense team," says one of the young lawyers who had offered his services. "It was obvious from the outset that this was going to be a high-profile case and that it would present some very knotty and exciting legal issues. But I suppose I always knew one of the big guns would get it."

Although Joseph Kelner announces at once that he will charge no fee for his services, there's soon little doubt that the payoff will come in other ways, not least of them more public notice and attention than he normally could have expected in a lifetime.

True, he has had celebrated cases and important positions before. He is a past president of the American Trial Lawyers Association. He was one of the lawyers for the Kent State University students in their civil suits stemming from shootings by the Ohio National Guard in 1970. But by and large, the kind of negligence and personal injury law he has practiced until now doesn't make headlines the way criminal law does.

Even in criminal law, however, the visibility this case provides is almost unprecedented. From the day his appointment is announced, when Joseph Kelner speaks of anything even remotely connected to his most famous client, his words are broadcast to a waiting world.

For Kelner, there's something else as well. Himself the victim of two muggings—once, as he tells it, with a "cocked pistol to my heart," the other when he was beaten unconscious—his identification with Bernie is immediate and profound. "We share an important bond; we're both mugging victims," he explains at a press conference in his lower Broadway office when he announces that he will represent Goetz. "Only if you've been mugged can you know that feeling. It's a bond that develops between two people who have both seen everything worth living for put on the block."

Undoubtedly this shared experience and the intensity of Kelner's feeling about it is crucial in helping Bernie to choose him above the others. For Bernie, the knowledge that his anger is understood, that his passion is shared, that he has found a companion in his crusade against street crime, can only be immensely reassuring. Moreover, Kelner's unquestioning belief that his actions were just undoubtedly gives Bernie some relief from the kind of internal doubt and ambivalence that were apparent in his earlier conversations, whether with Myra Friedman or with the police, when he slipped between self-justification and describing his act with words like "cold-blooded," "vicious," and "savage."

At the same time, Kelner, old enough to be Bernie's father,

can become his surrogate, easing the pain of betrayal and loss with which the son has lived for so long. Unlike his own father, this one promises not to inflict pain but to save him from it. This father embraces him unconditionally, honors him uncritically. This father promises to share his vision of the world, to help him make it a reality, not to threaten its very foundations.

Like Bernie, Kelner attacks the criminal justice system and excoriates the courts for becoming a revolving door through which criminals are sent back on the streets with little concern for public safety. Like Bernie, he rages at the injustice of that system which, he says, grinds up a man like his client while leaving his alleged assailants to go free. Like Bernie, he reviles the youths who were shot with every epithet in the book.

But as the boundaries between himself and his client become blurred for Kelner, and the two seem increasingly to become one, his ability to manage the case objectively becomes at least somewhat impaired. Certainly he's concerned about crime in the streets, about the failures of the criminal justice system; certainly he wants to see the kinds of changes that would make us all feel safer. But it's equally certain that his identification with his client, and the intensity of emotion he brings to the case, is born of personal affront, not his abhorrence of some abstraction called "the system."

In avenging Bernie Goetz, Joe Kelner avenges himself. This is his chance to retaliate against those who have victimized him, to reorder his immediate world in a way that feels safe and predictable once again. Not the internal setting to permit the objectivity needed to manage so complicated and difficult a case as this one soon proves to be.

It isn't *just* for the publicity, then, that Kelner seems to take every opportunity to appear on radio, television or in the newspapers, to accept lecture engagements to talk about the issues the case has raised, to journey to Washington to give testimony before a congressional committee investigating crime. He has a task to do, a message to convey. And Bernie Goetz is the medium.

But Joe Kelner is also a conscientious professional who has at least some sense of his own limitations. So to handle the complex criminal aspects of the Goetz affair, he recruits Barry Slotnick, a phenomenon in the world of criminal lawyers who, in 1981, was voted the nation's outstanding attorney in criminal law by the *American Lawyer*.

Slotnick's large legal staff, housed in impressive offices in lower Manhattan, engage, in his words, "solely and exclusively in criminal law." Unlike Kelner, he makes no public statement about fees. Instead, when questioned he says flatly, "My fee arrangements are not matters for public attention and discussion."

Kelner and Slotnick, whose names will soon be so closely linked they're spoken almost as one, are an oddly mismatched pair with whom the fates have dealt unevenly. Kelner, square of build, medium in height, ponderous in style, somewhat gravel-voiced and pompous in speech, is a man of little personal grace or charm. The already coarse features on his heavy-jowled face are coarsened further by his excess weight. His indifferent attire does little to hide the slack body beneath.

Slotnick is the perfect opposite. Gifted with a natural grace that characterizes both his physical appearance and his personal style, Barry Slotnick is a tall, slender, elegantly tailored man. As if on order to match the rest of him, even the beard that rings his handsome face shows just the right touch of gray. His words flow easily and fluently; his gaze is direct and disarmingly open, offering warmth, beckoning trust. "The only reason I win cases," he says, flashing his quick smile, "is because I get a jury to trust me."

Are they each what they seem to be? Probably not. In other circumstances, perhaps when he's less personally involved with the issues in a case, Joe Kelner may be less pompous, less rigid, less unyielding than the man now on public view. And Barry Slotnick's easy charm and winning ways are clearly part of the same highly polished, well-executed performance with which he has charmed juries so successfully. Any criminal lawyer—especially one whose clients have included some of the country's most renowned mobsters—who, in his own words, "went for twelve years without losing a jury trial" must be a tough and ruthless adversary, willing to use anything short of the illegal in the service of winning.

Yet, despite the outer accoutrements of his success, there's something of the boy from the Bronx still present in Slotnick. Although he's come a long way from those early years in an Orthodox Jewish family, he seems still to be looking over his shoulder and saying to himself, "Can this really be me?" Like the nouveaux riches, he can't quite believe in his achievements, isn't certain anyone will notice if he doesn't show them off. So his talk is peppered with reminders of his accomplishments— getting *certiorari* in the United States Supreme Court, landmark cases fought and won, his chauffeured limousine, his home in a posh suburb of the city.

At the outset, his interest in the Goetz case was strictly professional, he says, just another case that looked like an interesting one. Reminiscing about his entry into it, he recalls, "I didn't really understand the magnitude of the case until the day it was announced that I was to be Mr. Goetz's attorney. I was in the Southern District Federal Court and when I got out for lunch, there were hundreds (it seemed like thousands) of reporters out there. The Sharon and Westmoreland cases were being heard there then, so I thought they must be waiting for them. But then they descended on me. I'm used to handling high-profile cases and getting lots of press attention, but I've never seen anything like it—never ever."

On the surface, the Kelner–Slotnick alliance looks like a heaven-sent match: Two top-notch lawyers, one to handle the civil side of Bernie Goetz's troubles, the other to take charge of the criminal side. Yet the very qualities that have made each of them a success in their chosen specialty will soon also make it difficult for them to work easily together as equal teammates.

Both are men accustomed to control, to planning the strategy of a case unhindered, to making decisions that others will carry out. They may turn to colleagues to discuss a thorny legal problem, to try out a theory or a set of tactics. But the final decisions generally have been theirs alone. Now they find themselves in a situation where they must turn to each other not only for advice but for consent as well. And paradoxically, in a case where the immediate need is for criminal expertise, Joe Kelner, the civil lawyer, is chief counsel.

No one talks openly about their difficulties; the case is too important to be jeopardized. But as the complications arise, as the publicity surrounding the case escalates and is perpetuated by the public presence first of Joseph Kelner, then of Bernie Goetz himself, Barry Slotnick becomes restive and cautiously displays some of his discontent. Thus, some months later, he reflects upon a set of events highly unfavorable to his client and says, in a barely veiled reference to Kelner, "The problem is that some others became very self-important, and I got pushed to do things I'm not at all happy about." With a knowing look, he adds, "You're pretty smart; you can figure out who I'm talking about."

On the prosecution side, while assistants may try the case—first Susan Braver, later Gregory Waples—the decision maker and, therefore, the one who counts is District Attorney Robert Morgenthau. When the Goetz case came to public attention, Morgenthau had already been in office for ten years and was widely respected as, in the words of a *National Law Journal* article, "running one of the sharpest and most prestigious local prosecutor's operations in the nation." And in a New York *Times* profile, published at the height of the furor surrounding the subway shootings, the author wrote: "Mr. Morgenthau, now in his 11th year in office, has been often quoted but seldom criticized." But in the Goetz affair, he will soon find himself widely criticized and sorely tested.

This slim, patrician, bespectacled, gray-haired son of former United States Secretary of the Treasury Henry Morgenthau has devoted much of his adult life to public service. At sixty-five, he's smaller than expected, partly perhaps because the name he bears is itself so large, partly because in photographs and on camera he carries an air of authority that's less present in person.

Indeed, even in his almost overwhelmingly large but tasteful office, his quiet, dignified manner, his capacity to look fully attentive, make him seem easily approachable. It's only from some distance that one understands fully how carefully measured the interaction has been.

Although he demurs and downplays his influence, it's no secret in the city that he has enormous political clout, especially in matters relating to the criminal justice system. Becoming an assistant to Robert Morgenthau is like a career insurance policy. A former campaign manager now sits on the federal bench. Ten others who today occupy federal judgeships served as Morgenthau's assistants when he was the United States Attorney from 1961 to 1970, as did Representative Charles Rangel and former Police Commissioner Robert McGuire.

Two hundred and fifty former assistants are members of the Robert M. Morgenthau Association. The membership roster of this group, which meets twice each year, resembles a Who's Who of federal, state and local judges and other public officials, and includes partners in many of the city's top law firms as well as officers of some of its largest corporations and foundations.

Like all the other attorneys in the case, Morgenthau, too, deplores the fact that it has become a media circus. With some, it's clear that they helped to make it that way. Others have been reluctantly dragged along by the insatiable media demands and their own fear about what will be said if the press and the cameras are not fed something, anything. "If you don't give answers, you create hostility," Mark Baker, an associate of Barry Slotnick, tells a *National Law Journal* reporter. "There is an incredible hunger for information, and if you don't feed it, it begins to turn on you."

Only one, Irwin Shaw, a Legal Aid Society lawyer representing Barry Allen, steadfastly but politely refuses to be drawn into the public fray and, perhaps by his own example, is successful in keeping his client quiet as well.

For some of these attorneys, the media attention is both flattering and seductive, at least at first. It's part of the kick and excitement of a high-visibility case. But Robert Morgenthau has little reason to seek such attention since it comes to him so readily. For him, it's not new to see his face on a television screen or on the front page of one of the city's newspapers. Yet, like the others, he finds himself entrapped by the voracious hunger of the press, whether print or electronic. If he's silent, the press "speaks" for him. If he speaks, he's accused by Kelner and Slotnick, along with others, of manipulating public opinion, of trying the case in the press.

For each of the attorneys, this case comes to have its own special meaning. For some a career is at stake, for some a reputation; for some it's their ideological and political commitments that compel them, for some their very sense of self. For Robert Morgenthau, less than a year away from what probably will be the last election campaign of his long and distinguished career, the case of Bernhard Hugo Goetz will soon call into question what until now has been a given: his competence as a prosecutor, his honor and integrity in the service of the law.

18· It was a scene Gertrude Goetz was to remember until she died in 1977, seventeen years later. As she would tell her daughter Barbara, she had made the final arrangements and was ready to leave the Institut auf dem Rosenberg, the elite boarding school in the village of St. Gallen in Switzerland where her two youngest children would spend the next several years. But her small son was not ready to be left. In a panic, he clutched at her departing figure. "Mommy, mommy, please don't leave me," he pleaded tearfully, as she disengaged herself and walked quickly away, his terrified voice resounding inside her long after she was out of earshot.

It was a long time before Bernie was able to adjust to his new life. He wrote his mother very often, especially at first, and she went over to visit him frequently. The classroom work, no matter how difficult, was never a problem. It was the hours outside that were so hard for him, the hours when studying was done, when there was nothing more to immerse himself in, or when he was too tired to do so. It was then that this isolated, asocial child suffered for want of the comfort of home and family.

Years later, when asked how he felt about those years in boarding school, Bernie replies with one of his characteristic enigmatic statements which he typically refuses to elucidate, "Switzerland opened my eyes to a lot of different things." Was he picked on there as he had been in Rhinebeck? He now says philosophically, "I accept that it's part of human nature for some people to attack the weakest. . . . I may have had it worse than others, but others had it worse than me."

But what is viewed philosophically at thirty-eight can have tragic proportions at twelve. At that time, there would have been no way to understand why he had been banished, why he had to suffer alone. He had already lived through the scandal that rocked Rhinebeck and the surrounding communities at his father's arrest. He had already endured the agony of the trial, of sitting in the courtroom every day while the whole town watched and listened. After all that, being sent away could have made no sense to him.

In some families, usually those in the upper class where boarding school is part of the way of life, children are prepared for such departures for years. For those children, there's nothing unique about leaving home at a tender age; it's an accepted part of the world they live in. They may still suffer the moment when it comes, may still have some emotional difficulty in making the necessary adjustment. But at least they have always known it was coming, not just for them but for the friends and relatives around them.

For young Bernie, none of this was true. In his life, there was no expectation of boarding school, no preparation, no culture within which he was embedded that would have made his adaptation easier. Except for his father's arrest, he undoubtedly would have remained at home until he went off to college, just as his older siblings had done. For him, the rupture in the fabric of his life came with a suddenness that could only have been shattering almost beyond endurance. As shattering as the death of Ronald Cabey was to his son Darrell.

For a child just on the threshold of the transition between childhood and adolescence, the timing couldn't have been worse. He already had reason to distrust a world that had not treated him kindly. Now he had to suffer what could only have felt like the ultimate betrayal. And by the only people he had ever trusted.

Gertrude and Bernhard Goetz undoubtedly believed that the children would be better off away from the scene. The trial and Bernhard's conviction didn't end the matter. There were years of appeals that would keep it alive for them. Each time another action was taken in the courts, the community would be reminded as well. The older children were already away at college. Certainly it must have seemed prudent to protect young Bernie and his sister from anything more than they had already suffered.

But reasonable as it may seem to adults, the child can only wonder: Why are they sending me away? No matter what the parents' motive, no matter what the explanation, somewhere inside lives the question: What did I do? And all too often, the only answer the young mind can fathom is: I'm not good enough, lovable enough. They don't really want me.

Yet who could he blame? Not his father surely. The family myth of father's innocence could not be tampered with. And mother? Nobody—not she, not even the whole town of Rhinebeck—could stand up to his father. She could never protect him from his father's cruel criticisms and harsh rages, so he couldn't really expect her effective intervention now either. She, at least, came to visit and continued to express her love and concern, even if he couldn't always believe in it. To get angry at them, to allow himself to know it, could only lead to further isolation, greater desolation, increased guilt and fear.

But he would have had to blame someone, just as a parent must when a child gets into trouble. For a parent, it's not the child who's held responsible but those terrible friends. For Bernie, as for the rest of the family, there would also be a way out. It was not the father's behavior that was the cause of the pain and disruption; it was those lying punk kids who were his accusers.

For all of us, time brings some surcease from such pain. Scar tissue forms over the raw emotional hurt. We go on with our lives; we may even think we have, as we tend to say, "gotten over it." And in some ways we do. We repress, deny, sublimate —all defenses that are adaptive, all mechanisms without which none of us could survive. But especially when such painful experiences come to us at a tender age, these defensive maneuvers are also not without cost to the developing self—at the very least, cost in our ability to trust, to enter an intimate relationship again.

While Bernie was in school abroad, his family moved to Orlando, Florida. There, where the population of the region was exploding, his father once again invested in real estate in a suburb outside the city.

Whatever the cost to the family of those last years in Rhinebeck, they did nothing to diminish the senior Goetz's drive, resourcefulness or resilience. Instead, like the phoenix, he arose from the ashes to grow more powerful and stronger than ever. This time, it wasn't three houses he built, it was 1,100. And they weren't the modest homes of Wynkoop Lane on the edge of Rhinebeck. Instead, the homes in Park Manor, as the development is called, were built to sell for prices ranging from $75,000 to $90,000, a small fortune in the mid-1960s.

It was here that the family wealth was consolidated, here that Mr. Goetz turned his modest fortune into a large one, here that the family was living when Bernie and Bernice graduated from their Swiss high school and came home in 1964. It's here also that Bernice still lives as she continues in the active management of the development company her father started. Bernie, who would be caught in a love-hate conflict with his father until

he died twenty years later, would be a sojourner in his family
from then on.

The first contest between father and son came immediately
upon Bernie's homecoming. He arrived with the long hair that
was fashionable with students of the 1960s, a style to which his
father objected strenuously. But Bernie would not be moved. It
wasn't until he left home again, this time to spend a year at the
Christian Brothers school in Poughkeepsie, New York, that he
did for the Brothers what he would not do for his father. He
got a haircut.

After a year of living once again in the rural environment of
his childhood, Bernie left the country for the city. This time
he was headed for college—engineering school at New York
University's Bronx campus, just a few miles from the site of
Claremont Village, the home of the youths with whom his life
would one day become entwined.

The campus, set on a bluff overlooking the Harlem River
at the western edge of the Bronx, no longer exists. For decades,
its parklike setting, its quiet seclusion, was a haven for the
upwardly mobile immigrant kids who lived on the city streets
close by. Standing as it did in the middle of their narrow and
restricted world, it became for many of them a symbol of the
possible, the American dream right before their eyes, right under
their feet.

But the neighborhood changed. Just as the Bronx had held out
the promise of a better life for several generations of immigrants
and their children, for a short while it seemed to represent a
step up for black families from Harlem. As whites who made it
moved out—to Queens, to the suburbs of Long Island and
Westchester—blacks moved in. But what for whites had been
part of the climb, for blacks became the end of the line.

By the time Bernie Goetz arrived at this Bronx campus of
NYU in 1966, it was close to its demise. Its location in the heart

of a black ghetto at a time when racial tensions were on the rise would soon make it impossible to recruit students or faculty to what was a very expensive, essentially all-white private school.

The more peaceful protests of the civil rights movement were, by then, on the wane. Instead, the sense of outrage and injustice of the black community was beginning to express itself all across the land in ways that were far more dangerous both to self and to society. There were no more songs, no more freedom marches, no more black hands linked in comradeship with whites. In their place were firebombs and shouts of "Honky, go home!"

Harlem, just a few miles south of the campus, had already exploded in rage. Before Bernie would finish his schooling on this white island in the middle of a neighborhood turned black, Watts, the black ghetto of Los Angeles, had burned, to be followed not long after by Newark and Detroit. And white America was beginning to know the meaning of fear.

It surely would have been difficult for this young man who had grown up in bucolic white Dutchess County to find himself in the teeming heart of the black Bronx. The disjunction between his high-school years in a medieval cathedral town in Switzerland and an environment that was so hostile, that felt so unsafe, must have been unnerving. Yet in a peculiar way there must also have been something familiar about it.

Psychologically, Bernie had always been an alien, had always lived in a situation that had at least some elements of danger for him. Now he was choosing to do so again. True, in his earlier experience, it wasn't his physical safety for which he feared. But whether it's body or psyche under threat makes little difference, since they're not easily separable. It's not possible to scar the body without touching the soul. And it was the attacks on his psyche in childhood that helped turn Bernie's body in adulthood into what *Time* magazine has called "a human question mark."

Freud called this unconscious tendency to re-create the painful experience of the past a repetition compulsion. Sometimes we repeat the past because it's familiar. Painful though it may be, we know what to expect, know how to deal with it. Therefore, it feels safe—or at least safer than some unknown that might live in our imagination but is beyond our real comprehension. But a repetition compulsion can also be an attempt to master the old hurt through its reenactment, an unconscious need to relive the childhood situation in the hope that this time it will come out differently.

Sometimes it works. We choose a "mother" who protects us better than our real mother could, a "father" who is kind, people who see and accept us as we are. Most of the time, however, these re-creations are doomed to the same old ending because we bring to them the same "self" and choose people and situations that, whatever their surface qualities may seem to promise, underneath are the same as those from the past.

So it was for Bernie on this college campus in the Bronx. Whatever his conscious or unconscious fantasies may have been when he made the choice, the situation was a familiar one. He was once again confronted with the experience of being endangered. The threat of attack was an ever-present reality—the physical threat, yes, but equally unsettling, the threat of being humiliated, of being taunted by others when they sensed his fear. For Bernie Goetz, yet another layer of an old experience to feed the flames of rage and fear that were growing inside him.

19 · In the State of New York, a witness who testifies before a grand jury is granted automatic immunity from prosecution for the crime at hand. The witness can waive immunity, of course, but regardless of the crime, the prosecutor cannot compel anyone to do so. Once immunity from prosecution is conferred, however, a witness must testify or face the threat of contempt.

For the prosecution, the immunity issue has its own set of complications. If they permit someone to testify before the grand jury, they forsake the possibility of charging the witness with a crime. If they insist upon a waiver of immunity before the person's appearance, they may lose the very testimony they need to get the indictment they're after.

It's standard practice, therefore, for a deal to be made. The DA agrees to immunity for a lesser crime in exchange for testimony against someone who has committed a greater one. But in *People of the State of New York* v. *Bernhard Goetz*, the issue of immunity poses a giant headache for District Attorney Robert Morgenthau.

He knows his case against Goetz will be considerably strengthened with the testimony of the youths he shot. Yet from what he knows now, he can't be certain whether one crime was committed or two. Was a robbery in progress, stopped only by the bullets from Goetz's gun? Bernie says yes; the three youths still capable of talking say no.

Although they haven't been charged with anything and there's no indication they will be, the assumption that they were about to precipitate a mugging is widespread among New Yorkers. To allow these young men immunity from prosecution, the DA knows, is to give ammunition to those whose voices are now raised in a sharp attack on the criminal justice system for just such practices. So he asks them to waive their right to immunity.

Their attorneys insist they will not. Given the story Goetz has told, how do they know, the lawyers ask, that the boys won't be charged with attempted robbery? Unless they have immunity, there will be no testimony.

Morgenthau holds firm. He can't agree to immunity, he argues, because it might jeopardize the prosecution of other charges pending against them.

Nonsense, the lawyers retort; it's done all the time. There's no reason at all to fear that immunity in this case would carry over to any of the other crimes for which these youths have already been charged.

They're stalemated. The district attorney's position is fixed: No immunity. The lawyers for all four young men agree: No testimony. Ronald Kliegerman, attorney for James Ramseur, says emphatically, "The overriding factor for me is that my client will not testify without immunity because I'm afraid they're going to try to nail him to the wall somehow." Howard Meyer, who represents Troy Canty, dismisses Morgenthau's reasoning impatiently. "It's politics," he asserts. "Normally it's not an issue. A person is called before the grand jury and immunity is automatic. But Morgenthau obviously doesn't want to confer immunity on these black kids who are being so vilified all over and who are being called thugs and punks and names like that."

The immunity debate rages in the press. Articles appear explaining the issues; people watch and listen. Men and women who never heard of immunity, who until recently had no idea what the concept meant, now take sides, some shouting "He should," others "He shouldn't."

On one side are those who take the "It's standard practice" position. The DA gives immunity every day of the week without all this concern about how it will affect charges pending against a witness, so why all the questions now? they ask. Even if a mugging was intended, it's a lesser crime than shooting down four people, they argue. Besides, the grand jury has the tapes and transcripts of Goetz's New Hampshire confession. So they've already heard his side of the story. If none of the other principals in the drama is heard, how can the jurors make a reasoned decision?

On the other side are the people who, like Bernie Goetz, are disillusioned and disgusted with the criminal justice system and demand reform. Sure, they shout bitterly, give the criminals immunity and crucify the victim. So long as we let criminals off easy like that, they insist, we'll never control crime in this country. How are we ever going to teach these damn kids—and all the others like them who have turned our cities into urban jungles—that crime doesn't pay? No immunity for those punks, they demand. Let 'em fry!

Morgenthau's position remains unaltered. Immunity is out of the question. The speculation around the courts is that he's afraid of this case because of the intensity of public response it has stirred. His upcoming campaign for reelection could stand or fall on whether he's seen as soft on criminals like these youths. He's stung by the charges that fly all around, but he responds coolly.

Sitting easily in his large, comfortable chair behind a huge desk, the district attorney spells out the complications of the immunity law in New York. Confining the immunity to the case at hand isn't as simple and easy as some people are now trying to make it seem, he insists. Unlike most other places, New York offers *transactional immunity*, which, he explains, protects a person from prosecution for *any* crime mentioned during the immunized testimony. So if a person testifying about one crime mentions his or her involvement in another one, that second crime may well be covered by the immunity that's been granted in the case being heard.

As an example, he talks about a case in which a woman under indictment for selling heroin was also a witness in an unrelated murder case. When she went before the grand jury, Morgenthau says, they asked her to talk about the events of the day of the murder. She was evasive. As the conversation took its twists and turns, she was asked what she did for a living. She replied that she used to sell heroin until she was arrested.

His voice rises in intensity and he leans forward in his chair: "Now remember, they were not investigating narcotics at all, only a murder to which she was a witness. And no one asked her about the narcotics charge. Yet because it came up in the course of the interrogation about the murder, she was given automatic immunity on the heroin indictment."

Other experts in criminal law scoff at the DA's explanation. The transactional immunity of New York has some problems, they agree, but it's not exactly as the DA tells it. Unlike this type of immunity in other places, the New York law protects against the very possibility he's talking about. In a discussion about transactional immunity and its problems, Charles Whitebread, a leading authority on criminal procedure, confirms this view. "Often, witnesses given transactional immunity will testify about matters far beyond the subject of the questions asked in order to 'bathe' themselves in immunity. . . . New York, which still has transactional immunity, immunizes only answers which are responsive to the questions asked."

"Prosecutors are plenty wary," explains a well-known criminal lawyer. "It isn't as if someone can get up there and talk about other charges and they get automatic immunity. That's nonsense. It only works that way if the prosecutor asks the wrong questions. They manage to play it safe in other cases, so what are they so afraid of in this one? It's not the law he's worried about; it's his political future."

His decision is not a political one, Morgenthau continues to insist. He's just doing his job. That job, as he sees it, includes subpoenaing three of the four victims of Goetz's gun to appear before the grand jury. The fourth, Darrell Cabey, not yet in a coma, is, nevertheless, too ill to be moved from his hospital bed.

Morgenthau knows the youths will refuse to waive immunity. But the charade is played out. On the afternoon of January 8, Barry Allen, Troy Canty and James Ramseur are each brought before the grand jury. To each of them, Susan Braver, the prosecutor handling the case, puts a single question: "Do you wish to waive immunity?" One by one they reply that, on advice of counsel, they do not.

From January 15, when the subject is first raised, until January 25, when the grand jurors will finally render their verdict, everyone waits for Bernie Goetz to make good his offer to appear before the grand jury. Despite his statement on Wednesday, January 16, that he's ready to walk out of his apartment to "seek justice with his head held high," he's nowhere in sight.

But Kelner keeps him in the news with statements to the press and appearances on television. In an interview on ABC's *Good Morning America*, he tells host David Hartman that since Bernie "has nothing to hide," both he and his client are "leaning" toward testifying. At a press conference soon after, he elaborates: "If he [Bernie] had his way he would have held a full-scale press conference the day of his surrender and told the world everything that happened. . . . He doesn't want to duck anyone. He says he wants to look the world square in the eye. But from a defense point of view, talking too much doesn't make sense."

A day or so later, he talks again to reporters and reminds them that Bernie Goetz "cast aside any attempt to be devious" when he turned himself in to the police in Concord. "It may be to his advantage," he says, "to continue that display of honesty by testifying to the grand jury."

What he doesn't say, of course, is that this "display of honesty" came after Goetz already knew the police were looking for him, as he was to acknowledge to a reporter some time later. "If you had known you were not being sought, would you still have turned yourself in?" she asked him. "Good question," replied Bernie. "Nope."

In a quieter vein, on the day after headlines proclaim Bernie's desire to appear before the grand jury—the same day he talks about walking out of his apartment with "head held high"—he and Kelner appear in court with a petition for the videotapes of Goetz's New Hampshire confession. "It is my duty," Kelner tells Criminal Court Judge Jay Gold, "to have access to those videotapes so that I can make an appropriate determination whether Mr. Goetz will testify before the grand jury." Assistant DA Susan Braver objects. "The matter is before the grand jury and this is not the appropriate time," she argues. Judge Gold agrees with the prosecution; Kelner's motion is denied.

Joseph Kelner leaves the Criminal Court building angrily, announcing that he will decide "next Monday or Tuesday at the latest" whether he will allow his client to testify. The district attorney says he'll wait until Monday for the decision. In the ponderous style that is by now so familiar, Kelner tells a *Post* reporter, "His [Goetz's] sense of fairness of mind is somewhat offended by the fact that we're not going to be permitted to view those tapes or statements before he goes before the grand jury."

As the maneuvering between prosecution and defense continues, the grand jury's deliberations are stalled. There's nothing more they can do until they're notified about whether Bernie will testify.

As for the public, interest in the case continues to burn brightly, but the secrecy with which grand jury proceedings have historically been cloaked leaves most questions unanswered. What witnesses does the prosecution have? What evidence has Ms. Braver presented? Everyone knows about the taped confession made in New Hampshire, and it's assumed that it has been presented to the grand jurors. But officials there and in New York aren't talking about what's on the tapes.

Concord's Police Chief Walchak explains politely that he has promised the New York DA there will be no leaks from his department. New Hampshire's Assistant Attorney General Isaac refuses to discuss the tapes, saying, "The evidence should come out in a proper legal fashion." By which he means in a trial court. And, of course, the Manhattan district attorney's office is equally silent. "It's against the law to talk about evidence being presented to the grand jury," responds Morgenthau to every request for information.

The legal instructions that have been or will be given to the jurors are also the subject of intense interest. Since, according to New York's law on justifiable homicide, the line between excessive or unnecessary force and self-defense is dependent on a person's *perception* of a threat, a subway rider surrounded by four teenagers asking for money, as Bernie claims he was, could justifiably defend himself with a gun if he *reasonably believed* he was about to be hurt or killed. With a law as ambiguous as this one, the lay women and men of the grand jury will have to rely even more heavily than usual on the legal interpretations and instructions of the prosecutor in coming to a determination in the case.

20· At college, Bernie consolidated his lifelong interest in electronics and majored in nuclear engineering, one of only four students in his graduating class of 450 to specialize in the field. It was a choice that seemed to make psychological sense for him. It would be safe, predictable, dependable—an occupation that held out the promise of certainty, that required only the right calculations to make something come out the way he wanted it to. Not like trying to deal with people or to understand them; not like having to depend on them either.

But, unfortunately for him, even engineers have colleagues with whom they must work collaboratively, and supervisors whose authority they must accept. Bernie was good at neither of these. So after graduation, when he entered the world of work, he found himself in trouble again. His compulsively perfectionist standards, his insistence that there was only one right way, his inability to tolerate a dissenting point of view, his refusal to accept the authority of his supervisors, either got him fired or forced him to quit every job he had.

In his first job as a test engineer for Westinghouse Electric Corporation, for example, he would unilaterally decide that some part on the nuclear submarines the company was building didn't meet contract specifications, and he would inform the navy inspectors to that effect. Sometimes he was right to insist that an error had been made or a corner cut. Once he noticed that the hatch covers which protect the emergency shutoff switch for the nuclear reactor on the ship had no latch. Concerned, he warned company officials that this would present a serious hazard under combat conditions. But they paid no attention, retreating instead behind the excuse that the contract didn't call for a latch. Angrily, Goetz pored through the navy manuals until he found an obscure regulation requiring all hatch covers to have latches, and forced the company to latch the hatch.

Often, however, he was unable to discriminate between those things that merited attention and concern and those that did not, indeed between what was actually a flaw in the equipment and what simply didn't measure up to the criteria of perfection he himself had set. In all these matters, the contradictions that are so much a part of Bernie Goetz were never far from the surface. On the one hand, there was this insistence on "going by the book." On the other, he had no problem in violating "the book" when he decided *he* knew a better way. So while he would press his employer to abide by the rules as he saw them, he saw no reason why he shouldn't break them when *he* decided it made sense.

Thus, when a plumber, who was needed to complete some work on one of the subs, was not immediately available, Bernie did the job himself—in violation of company and union rules. When he was censured by both management and union officials, he couldn't understand why they were so angry. He had, after all, only done what needed doing. *He* knew he could do it as well as any plumber, so why all the fuss?

In 1971, about a year after he received his degree in nuclear engineering, weeks after he lost his first job in the field, Bernie accepted his father's offer to join his Park Manor Development Company in Florida and become a builder of houses. In doing so, Bernie returned to a father who had betrayed the family trust, whose behavior had cost his son dearly. But it clearly was something he had to do. The child who was sent from the family so long before he was ready needed to try to go home again.

What was he looking for when he went back into the fold? Surely he wanted to feel once more the warmth of the family setting, the love of his mother. Without doubt, he wanted to be reassured about his place in her heart. But he could have had all that without joining his father in business. His sister Barbara explains his decision by saying simply, "His dad needed him; he wanted to please his dad." An important truth, but surely not the whole of it.

It's a common phenomenon that the parent who is more distant, the one from whom the child cannot get what she or he wants or needs, remains a central and unresolved figure in the internal life of the adult. With some people the conflict is obvious. They will take the "good" parent for granted while spending years of their adult lives trying to please the one they're less certain of, to draw him or her close. Others who, on the surface, seem to have separated themselves from the offending parent, nevertheless unconsciously choose lovers or mates with whom they will replay the old parental script, always wanting something they can't get, always feeling angry and deprived when they don't get it.

There's not much doubt that there was this kind of unfinished business between father and son, that Bernie needed a sign of love and approval from his harsh and distant father. And in this case, there was also another dimension to the son's unresolved internal conflicts. As he struggled, as all adolescent boys must, with his developing sense of himself and his maleness, the issues of sexuality and identity would have been even more difficult for him than for the ordinary teenager. The dilemma he would have faced is this: If he identified with his father, he couldn't be certain that his own emerging sexual feelings would not also lead him to dangerous behaviors. If he renounced that identification, he would suffer guilt and anxiety—guilt, because it would seem to the boy that he had betrayed his father; anxiety, because he would be left at this tender age without a strong and positive male figure in his internal life.

By joining his father in his life's work, he could at least hope to find the identification he had sought during those earlier years. If he could identify with him, become one with him, he might win the approval he longed for so deeply. Finally, he could be safe and at peace, could quiet the voices inside him, still the doubts. Not just about his father but about himself as well.

But it wasn't destined to be. His wishes and fantasies, conscious and unconscious, would never come true. Father and son came together over a past that had already molded them and the relationship in ways that were not easily reversed. The elder Bernhard hadn't changed. By adulthood, his son had built a fortress of defenses against this man who so often seemed like an enemy and who was, at the same time, such an important figure in his inner psychic life.

Unquestionably, Bernie's continuing problems with authority were born in childhood when he had to fight so hard to maintain some sense of his own integrity, his own autonomy. Similarly, the grandiose sense of himself that permitted the kind of behavior that got him fired from his job was part of a defense against the contemptuous devaluation his father had visited upon him so consistently. No matter how much he might have yearned for his father's love and approval, Bernie could not have dropped these defenses readily. Nor was it likely that his father would make it easy for him to do so.

Consequently, their reunion was a setup for unremitting conflict, almost always over the same issue. Speaking of this period, Barbara explains that Bernhard Sr. "liked to cut corners," while Bernie always wanted "to do things right." So time and again, father and son fought. Bernie argued for the finest materials, the most perfect house; his father insisted on what he called a more moderate and realistic approach and, not incidentally, one that would be more profitable as well. That the houses were being built in accordance with local building codes and specifications was irrelevant to Bernie; he wanted them to be more and better.

Tension between the two men reached unbearable proportions. The son refused to bow to the authority of the father; the father overruled him every time. His brother-in-law, Norman Weinstein, now a psychiatrist in California but then working in the family business alongside father and son, recalls the many times that Bernie would hire a subcontractor whose work he could respect, only to have the father cancel the contract his son had signed. But Bernie never gave up. Just as he had fought his superiors at Westinghouse, so he fought his father. And for the same reasons. He wanted it done right, and only his definition of "right" would do.

There was undoubtedly some legitimacy to the manifest content of the arguments between father and son. But underlying it all was the struggle of two men, each intent on getting from the other what he would not, could not, give. For the father, it was the unquestioning obedience he felt was his due; for the son, the respect, admiration and approval he hungered for.

After four years, Bernie gave up the fight and left his father's business. It would be almost ten years before he spoke to his father again, and then for a deathbed reconciliation. Then it would be Bernie alone who would stand vigil over his father's last hours of life, he alone who would be there at the moment of his father's death—one more attempt to establish the connection he had been seeking all his life.

But not his last. He would continue to suffer the doubts and anxieties—about father, about self—until perhaps one day, with a blast from his gun, he would know finally he had become a man. A man who had avenged not just his own historic humiliations but his father's as well. But to do so, he would have to wait until his father was dead. Only with death and the idealization it permits, only when the father was no longer the living reminder of the rage the son had borne for so long, could the ideal father he sought become a fixed part of his internal life.

This isn't to say these feelings were present in consciousness when he confronted Barry, James, Troy and Darrell. Nor is it likely that he knew in the moment he pulled the trigger and couldn't stop shooting until his gun was empty that these shots were meant to avenge his father and to deliver retribution for his own suffering as well. But the conjunction of events is undeniable.

Bernhard William Goetz died in September 1984. Three short months later, in December, his son and namesake, Bernhard Hugo Goetz, mourning a loss that, in fact, had happened a quarter century earlier, walked into a subway train carrying a loaded gun, sat down next to four black teenagers and, at the first provocation, let loose with a barrage of bullets that would be heard around the world—bullets aimed at targets that existed as much in his past as in the present.

21 · On Friday, January 18, the media have a new field day as parts of the confession tapes are leaked. Unidentified sources familiar with the tapes are quoted as saying that Goetz never "expressed remorse about the shootings, that he said he felt he had done the right thing and that he wished he could have done more." One of the sources describes the statement as "rambling," saying he believes it "may not help him." Another says of Bernie Goetz, "He's no hero."

"I would have kept on shooting if I hadn't run out of bullets," Bernie is now quoted as saying. And in an apparent reference to Troy Canty, who allegedly asked him for five dollars, he's reported to have told police, "I should have gouged his eyes out with my car keys."

But Susan Braver revealed all this and more at the arraignment proceedings early in the month. Why does it become news now when these same facts were paid scant attention then?

It's certainly true that the hungry press needs news and will sometimes create it when it's not available. We've seen it happen repeatedly in recent years as crisis after crisis, from hostages to hurricanes, have been given the full media treatment, and television and newspaper reporters keep talking and writing long after they have run out of anything useful to say. In this case, there was plenty of excitement, plenty to write about early in the month without headlining these revelations. But it has been quieter lately, and reporters are pushed, by both internal need and external demand, to keep the media circus running.

Still, whether there are many or few, a choice is made about which facts to present—which to play up, which to play down. And now as then, there's the same kind of selective inattention to certain of the facts at hand. So, for example, a national public opinion poll taken during the week before these disclosures hit the headlines, but released afterward, shows 45 percent approving of Goetz's actions, 46 percent disapproving, 9 percent with no opinion. Not surprisingly, more men than women defend him: 51 percent to 39 percent. Since this is the first systematic national survey to be reported, there's no way to know with any certainty whether it reflects changing attitudes.

It does, however, seem startling. Only 45 percent of American adults approve the shootings, 46 percent *disapprove*. Given the widespread belief that the support for Goetz has been over-whelming, this would seem to be a surprising division of opinion, one that would be hot news. Yet these figures appear with little fuss and fanfare, relegated to the inside pages only. No stories to analyze them, none to reflect upon them, to examine what they mean in view of all the hurrahs and hosannas we've heard until now.

Certainly the ambivalence, reservations and fear of the dissenters should, could, would have been news. Yet from the beginning the media have paid little attention to the opposition point of view, contenting themselves with focusing on the out-pouring of support. One reason, perhaps, is that those who oppose the subway shooter have, from the outset, consistently spoken with a quieter voice. They knew they didn't like what he did, but often weren't sure how to defend their position, sometimes weren't certain they wanted to do so. Partly that's because, like

those who applauded Bernie Goetz from the start, they have seen
the havoc such youths have wrought, and they share the common
anger about the fear and tension that have become a part of
modern urban life.

But there was something frightening, also, in the intensity
of the public expression of rage, in the taken-for-granted quality
it had which assumed it was fully shared. It felt engulfing and
all-encompassing, as if there was no room for anything else—an
atmosphere created, in part at least, by the media's inattention
to the other side, by the lack of caution displayed there, by
which facts were reported, which were not.

In joining the celebration with so few words of reservation,
the media fed the belief that the public was of one mind in the
case. This gave permission for the kind of unrestrained combination of rage and glee that was so commonly heard, while it also
helped to mute the opposition voices. At the same time, those
who made the decisions about what to present served well the
current national search for easy answers—for eliminating the
gray areas of life, for a world where black and white are clearly
delineated, where we can tell at a glance the good guys from the
bad guys.

True, they were reflecting what they perceived to be the
public consciousness, a perception born of the fact that it so
nearly matched their own. But in the process, they also pene-
trated that consciousness and helped to frame it. In doing so,
they made the Goetz supporters bolder and the dissenters more
timid. "For a long time, you felt like it was looking for trouble
to say you were opposed to what Goetz did. It was like being
against motherhood and apple pie," recalls a Queens man. "So
you kept your mouth shut. Who needed the aggravation of
fighting with those people? They were crazy about this guy;
they didn't even care that he shot people in the back."

In not presenting the full and complex events and reactions
that surrounded the subway shootings, then, the media didn't

just report the story, they were part of it—shaping it and creating it by the choices they made along the way, while they themselves were also responding to the intense public reaction and their need to meet it. It is in such a process of reciprocal interaction that media and public serve and reinforce each other.

22. January 22—the deadline for Bernie's decision about whether he will testify before the grand jury. The day comes and goes without word. The next day, Kelner explains that he was prevented from meeting the deadline by a phone call from Goetz "five minutes before he was to have made a statement." As a result, he hurriedly asked the DA for a one-day delay. Morgenthau confirms that he granted Kelner's request. Bernie now has until 3:30 in the afternoon of January 23 to decide.

No one knows exactly what happened. Kelner still insists that Goetz wants to testify but says he wants to see the video-tapes first. Morgenthau remains firm in his refusal. Someone supposedly close to Goetz whispers that Bernie and Kelner are at odds about the whole issue, with Goetz more inclined to make the appearance than his lawyer is to have him do so. But so many self-serving statements have come out of the Goetz camp while Bernie himself remains locked away from public scrutiny, it's hard to know what to make of it.

The second deadline passes. Bernie Goetz does not appear before the grand jury. It's rumored that Kelner asked Morgenthau for another day's delay, a request that was denied. The next day Kelner holds a news conference and announces the decision not to testify. "We advised him not to [testify] and he has agreed," he tells the assembled reporters, even though Bernie "was inclined" to do so. He also asserts categorically once again that regardless of the charges "there will never be a plea of guilty in this case."

For the next two days, speculation is rampant. Each day the headlines announce that this is the day the grand jury will conclude its deliberations, only to find by day's end that they were wrong. Finally, Morgenthau's office puts an end to the guessing game. "The matter will be concluded tomorrow," the waiting world is told. Responding to reporters' questions a little while later, Slotnick says he's prepared for an indictment. "I would be delighted if it doesn't happen, but frankly, I'd be surprised."

Late Friday afternoon, January 25, the twenty-three men and women of the grand jury reach their verdict and inform the prosecutor. They have refused to charge Bernhard Goetz with assault or attempted murder. Instead they indict him on three charges of illegal gun possession—two misdemeanor charges stemming from an unlicensed .38 caliber revolver and a 9 millimeter semiautomatic Lüger found in his apartment, and one felony charge for illegal possession of the gun he used in the shootings.

"When the DA called me and told me that he got off with just a weapons charge, I couldn't believe it," chuckles Slotnick as he recalls the moment. "I said, 'Say it again'; I thought I heard him wrong."

23· From January 9, when Darrell falls into a coma, until March 7—two seemingly endless, shattering months—the Cabey family waits. Every day Shirley Cabey takes the long subway ride from the Bronx to Fourteenth Street in Manhattan; every day she walks through the corridors of St. Vincent's Hospital to her son's room; every day she sits at his bedside, touching him, talking to him, watching, waiting, praying.

She's a familiar figure in the hospital now. Nurses, doctors, other regulars on the floor, watch for her arrival, cheer her on as she passes through, offer her what warmth and comfort they can. "Everybody at St. Vincent's has been wonderful," she says. "The people there are real friendly. And they care about Darrell; you can tell. The doctors are doing everything they know how. And they always explain everything to me so that I'll know what's going on."

But the agony is hers alone. Hers and her family's. Her mother, her cousin, some others, have gathered around. Sometimes they help out with the other kids, making sure that they get home from school safely, that they have a decent meal in the evening if she can't get back in time. Sometimes they accompany her to the hospital, keeping her company, sharing her watch over Darrell.

The other children, especially the younger ones, are upset, confused and angry. Suddenly, the whole household has been turned upside down. They no longer know what to expect, when they'll see their mother again, what condition she'll be in when she comes home. "They've been through a lot, and they're hurting and angry. They're very, very angry," she says, her eyes brimming with tears. "It comes out when they see Mr. Goetz's picture in the paper or on the TV screen. My little daughter, she takes her little fist and hits the picture in the paper every time she sees it—just hits and hits it, like she can't stop."

She understands their rage; she has plenty of her own. But she's also frightened for them. How can she help them contain it, direct it, so that they don't do something foolish or dangerous? Something that will hurt them more than anybody else. "I try to talk to them. They're good kids; they listen. But what can I say to them that'd make any sense?"

Sitting by Darrell's bed every day leaves her plenty of time to think, to try to cope with the bitterness that sweeps over her as she contemplates his future. True, for this deeply religious woman, the fact that he's still alive is a gift from God. But now she has to keep reminding herself to be thankful for the gift, has to keep struggling against the rage that threatens to overwhelm her.

The hope she'd had that in losing the use of his legs Darrell would be more likely to "use his head" is gone now. The doctors have explained to her that he suffered a respiratory failure during which his brain was deprived of oxygen. If he lives, they've warned her, he'll be brain-damaged. No one knows for sure yet how serious the damage will be. They can't know until he awakens from the coma—that is, *if* he does. But they're not optimistic. They know it was long, too long, before they got him onto the respirator. So they expect the damage will be what they call "extensive and probably irreversible."

She watches over him apprehensively. He looks so fragile lying there like that. Even in the coma he seems to be having problems and suffering. He gets agitated and thrashes around a lot; and he has these peculiar sweats where he gets wet all over. It seems to calm him a little when she touches him. So she's always laying hands on him. And now there's a faith healer who comes to see him once a week, too, a woman who offered her services after reading about Darrell in the paper. Ever since she's been coming, he's been resting a little better.

She knows she shouldn't think about the future right now, but she can't help it. There's so much to worry her; it follows her around all the time. What will become of them all? Who's going to pay the hospital and doctor bills? She doesn't have any medical insurance, never could afford it. If Darrell lives, he'll need care for the rest of his life. *For the rest of his life!* It's hard to imagine it. How will she manage? Where will the money come from?

She thinks about her job. She'll be sorry to leave it. It was good for her to work; she liked it. It was hard work she was doing, making and serving food in a mental hospital. But she felt useful. And the money was nice, very nice. But she can't possibly earn enough to have someone take care of Darrell when he comes home.

She shakes herself. "Stop it! You don't even know if he's going to live, and you're worrying about what's going to happen when he comes home." But she can't stop thinking, planning, wondering. And anyway, he *will* come home. She has to believe that. She just knows the good Lord won't let her son die. So she has to plan for it. It's not fair to the hospital where she was working to let them keep holding her place when she doesn't know when or if she'll be able to come back. "I took a leave when this happened, but how long can I expect them to wait, especially when I don't know if I'll ever be able to go back?"

. . .

People have advised her to find a lawyer. Goetz, they remind her, must bear some responsibility for Darrell's condition. She knows she should do it, even that she has to do it. But, God, how she wishes she could just be left alone. She's tired, a deep, bottomless well of exhaustion that seems to have settled in her core. If she starts up with lawyers, it's more bother, more trouble, more things to worry about and think about.

As it is, she can't stop thinking about the shooting, picturing it, trying to understand it, to make some sense out of the horror her son now faces. No matter how she turns it over in her mind, the same useless thought keeps gnawing at her: "He didn't have to shoot; even if the boys were bothering him, *he didn't have to shoot.*"

Just before Darrell fell into the coma, he told her he never said a word to Goetz except to plead with him not to shoot. "Man, why you gonna to shoot me for? I didn't do nothin' to you." He knew he shouldn't have been there, she says. But he also knew he didn't do anything to merit getting shot. In fact, Bernie himself told the police that, after he started to shoot at the others, Darrell "kinda stood up and . . . held the hand strap . . . pretending he wasn't with them." And an eyewitness testified before the grand jury that, when Bernie fired the second shot at Darrell, he was just "sitting there with his arms at his side."

"There's so much crime and people have stood for so much, I can understand that they're mad," says Mrs. Cabey. "You work all week for your little bit of money, and they take it away. That's very hurtful. But when somebody comes and asks for five dollars, there's other ways. You can walk to another car, or you can say no. You don't have to take out a gun and shoot four people.

"I guess I'm bitter because he's walking around and everybody's saying he did right. I just don't think Mr. Goetz should be free as a bird and everybody talking like he's a hero. How can they make him out a hero when he shot two boys in the back and had those dumdum bullets in his gun. That's why Darrell has so much damage; it was those dumdum bullets."

At first, she got only hate mail—terrible letters filled with racial epithets and expressing glee that her son was so badly wounded, letters that wished him dead, that threatened his life if he ever got well enough to walk the streets again. She talks about them with an astonishing calm, given the messages they carry. "I didn't know people could be so mean, but I made up my mind I wouldn't let them upset me. So after I read it, I'd take all the hate mail and stick it in between the pages of the Bible and say, 'The good Lord will take care of you.' "

That's changed now, and "the nice mail is pouring in"— letters from people who offer consolation, sympathy, support, encouragement. "So many people have been so wonderful, getting in touch like that. I feel like I have all these new friends. With all the support and love around me now, I can't be filled with hate."

Still it's clear she's torn. She's a God-fearing, forgiving woman. But she can't forgive Bernie Goetz. She doesn't want to be bitter and angry, fights against it much of the time, knows it's not the Lord's way. But it's a struggle she loses almost as often as she wins. Sometimes she can keep her pledge to herself to stay on the bright side of things, to keep the love in her heart instead of the hurt and the hate. Then she looks at her son, sees his frail body gripped with suffering even in his coma-tose state, and the rage boils up inside her. She reads the stuff in the papers, all the concern about how bad it will be for Bernie if Darrell dies, and she can't help wanting to scream, "What about me? What about my son?"

She's always been a very private person, but ever since the shootings, there's been all this publicity, reporters waiting at the hospital, at her house. As time goes on and everyone else involved in the case has something to say, she begins to feel that she must speak, too. The lawyers she finally hires encourage her to give some interviews, make some public statements in her son's behalf. So she becomes something of a public presence for a while. "I don't like all this publicity and attention. I'd be very happy to sit in the background somewhere and be nice and quiet. But the other people involved all can talk for themselves, but not my son. He can't talk. So I guess I have to do the talking for him."

At first, she's frightened of being recognized because of the threats she has received. So she's seen only from the back or in silhouette on the television screen. Her voice is heard defending her son, talking about his condition, insisting that Bernie must be punished. "I'm trying to help Darrell the best way I can by doing this," she says wearily, "but I don't know; I just don't know. I wouldn't wish any of this on anybody; it's a terrible lot to go through."

On March 7, Darrell Cabey awakens from his coma. For all her vigil of these last two months, his mother isn't there when he opens his eyes. The hospital staff decide not to telephone her with the news, choosing instead to surprise her. When she arrives at the hospital later in the day, she finds Darrell propped up in bed.

Out of the coma! She can hardly believe her eyes. Overcome with joy, she stands there gaping, unable to speak for a moment. He turns his head, looks at her and smiles. Then laughing and crying at once, she puts her arms around her son and holds him tightly to her breast. "I thought maybe he was trying to say something, but he had the respirator in. I was so thrilled to death that I was in there a half hour hugging him."

Shirley Cabey forgets her troubles for a while. Darrell's awake; he's going to live. The doctors had told her if he didn't come out of the coma in twelve days, there wouldn't be much hope. They were wrong. Maybe they'll be wrong again about the brain damage. God has answered all her prayers until now. Who knows what He'll do next? At least she can hope. Thank you, Lord, thank you.

Once the doctors are convinced that Darrell is stable, he's taken off the respirator. Despite constant monitoring and testing, the doctors still can't tell how extensive the brain damage has been and what, if any part of it, is reversible. Speech comes slowly. With painful effort over several weeks, he finally manages to say some words, not clearly yet, but it's progress. They soon learn that he has total amnesia about the shooting, remembers nothing from that time until after he awakened from the coma. More than two months gone absolutely blank. Since he can barely speak, there's no way to determine how much else has been blotted out of his mind as well.

They do know, however, that he has trouble remembering events in the present as well as those from the past. Even experiences repeated daily aren't easily retained. A word learned in the morning will be forgotten by afternoon. Each day he repeats his doctor's name; each day for a whole month he forgets it again.

As the months wear on and his efforts produce such small results, the stress begins to tell. He becomes frustrated and withdrawn. His mother tries to cheer him, but it's hard. What can she say that will help? What can she promise? No one knows what the nature and extent of the damage is; no one knows if he'll ever get one whit better than he is right now. She tries to keep her own hopes up, appeals to God not to let her slide. Not now, when she needs her faith so badly. Not now, when it's all she can offer her son.

Meanwhile, Darrell's attorney Ronald Kuby requests that the armed robbery charges that were pending against him before the December shootings be dropped, arguing that he is no longer mentally competent to participate in his defense. On September 12, 1985, nine months after he was shot, the Bronx DA's office agrees. "According to his doctors," a spokeswoman for the district attorney announces, "Darrell Cabey is permanently paralyzed and has the mental capacity of an eight-year-old. For him to be under indictment at this point would serve no purpose of justice."

24· During the same four years that Bernie and his father were locked in struggle, Bernie entered and left a marriage that, in its own way, was as unsatisfactory and turbulent as his relationship with his father. Her name was Elizabeth Boylan. He was attracted to her lively, outgoing style; she to his quiet, scholarly manner. An attraction of opposites that would soon cause difficulties for each of them.

They were married in a small private ceremony at his parents' home in Orlando. For the six months that followed, the newlyweds lived in that same house. It wouldn't have been an auspicious start for any new couple, but it was particularly difficult for this one because of the conflict between father and son.

But moving out wasn't easy either. Despite the senior Goetz's financial success, he paid his son a meager wage. So there wasn't much Bernie and Elizabeth could afford. When they finally did move into a home of their own, it was to a small apartment in a working-class area.

Bernie's twin passions for work and electronics dominated their lives. "He worked seven days a week . . . very, very, very long days," says his sister Barbara. A friend who knew them then says she felt sorry for Elizabeth because Bernie worked such long hours and took her for granted. When he wasn't working, he'd spend hours browsing in a store that sold electronic parts and equipment. Since he spent so much time there, the owner of that shop remembers well how Bernie would wander around, looking and touching, but rarely speaking. "He was an odd one," he recalls, "a man of very few words."

But it was more than the hours at work or his involvement in electronics that separated the young couple. Elizabeth wanted a more demonstrative, companionable and affectionate relationship with her husband. Even when he tried, however, Bernie simply didn't know how to give those things. "Bernhard could do things grindingly time-consuming," says his brother-in-law, Norman Weinstein. "When he did them, he was a nice, calm, comfortable conversationalist. But when he entered the world that other people know, he speeded up again and got nervous." His idea of a romantic gift, Weinstein recalled, was an electronic salt shaker with a stainless-steel telephone dial that controlled the amount of salt ejected. Dial 4, and four bursts of salt came out. "Elizabeth would rather have gotten roses," Weinstein concludes.

As the couple drifted apart, Bernie became suspicious of his wife, worrying about her activities outside the house, about her relationships with friends. In 1975, four years after they were married, he asked for a divorce. As one relative tells it, Elizabeth didn't really want to end their marriage. But Elizabeth herself is silent on the subject of both the marriage and the divorce, willing to say only, "He's a nice person. Good and kind and gentle."

With his marriage over and his hopes for a relationship with his father dead, there was nothing to keep Bernie in Florida any longer. Before the year was out, he had moved to New York.

When Bernie arrived in New York City in 1975, he rented an apartment on Christopher Street in Greenwich Village. There, after a rather lengthy period of unemployment, he established the business in which he still makes his living today—the Electrical Calibration Laboratory, Inc., a one-man operation run out of his apartment in which he tests and repairs complicated electronic equipment. Now finally, he began to put to use again both his long-standing interest in things electrical and some part of his training as an engineer.

Things went well for Bernie in New York. His business grew; he seemed to be happier than he had been for a long time. He spent many hours each week in the electronics stores on Canal Street, talking shop with the owners, helping customers solve problems. For the first time, he began to develop a social life— not close friends perhaps, but others who shared with him his single-minded absorption with electronics. These men—some of them the Canal Street storekeepers, others who, like Bernie, haunted the auctions and flea markets—appreciated the meticulous turn of his mind, the precision with which he approached a problem. "He explains something in electronics like he's reading out of an electronics book," says one admiringly.

It didn't matter to these new friends that Bernie was awkward socially, that he couldn't speak comfortably of anything but his work. It was all they, too, were interested in, all they, too, chose to talk about. "Getting into personal lives can break up a friendship," said one of these men. ". . . We talked shop talk, street-corner politics." With time, Bernie also talked more and more fervently about crime in the streets, obsessively going over the details of his own mugging, as he apparently tried to master the experience and deal with his rage at his treatment at the hands of the police, the licensing board that denied his application for a pistol permit, the courts that upheld the board's decision.

After a couple of years on Christopher Street, Bernie moved to his present address in an apartment in the front of the building. But the street noise on Fourteenth Street can be formidable, even in a city where people expect and accept plenty of commotion. So after a while, he moved to a rear apartment where his senses could get some respite from the assault. It was from this apartment that he ventured forth on that December day that unalterably changed his life. And it's here that he still lives and works.

Fourteenth Street. From Second Avenue to Seventh, it's still a shopping street, as it has been for several generations at least. But as the city changes, so does the character of the street.

Saturday has always been the big day on Fourteenth Street, the day when working people can take time to shop. Not so long ago, there was a babel of tongues to be heard there on a Saturday afternoon. Jewish, Italian, Irish and other immigrant parents, trailing their American children after them, spent the day looking over the wares. Sometimes they actually bought something—a pair of shoes for this child, a blouse for another, pants for a third. But often enough, they just looked, not because that was all they wanted to do but because looking was all they could afford.

The street, then as now, was filled with specialty shops, along with two larger stores—the famed S. Klein and Ohrbach's, the first volume discount merchandisers in the city. These are gone now, either moved uptown or disappeared entirely. But discounting remains the common way of doing business in the small shops that line the street, and prices are as negotiable as in any market south of the border.

People still come to Fourteenth Street to hunt for bargains. But there's no longer a polyglot of languages spoken there. Today it's like a Latin bazaar, with Spanish dominating the language of exchange. On a busy day, the sidewalk is jammed with shoppers and lookers, the merchandise spilling over the streetside bins that contained it before the customers arrived to pull it apart for examination.

Both Spanish and rock music blare from loudspeakers that hang outside music stores. When they quiet down for a moment, the stereos that seem to be permanently attached to every youth of

teenage years and above take over to make their contribution
to the noise that seems never to cease.

There's a good view of the action on Fourteenth Street from
the wide windows in the lobby of Bernie's building. Before ten
o'clock in the morning, it's relatively quiet out there on a
Saturday. The usual weekday morning traffic is still in bed. So
there aren't many cars speeding their passengers to work. And
the trucks that lumber up and down from Monday to Friday,
sometimes stopping to make a delivery and adding to the street's
congestion, are parked for the weekend.

The foot traffic, too, is quieter. Compared to the dizzying
weekday crowds who come pouring off the subway rushing to
work, it seems almost deserted. At this early hour on a Saturday,
there are only the occasional passersby and the usual assortment
of street people in view.

A white man, about fifty, stumbles by in an alcoholic haze.
A young Puerto Rican swings along, his stereo blasting. A thin,
pinched-faced white woman, shoulders hunched against the
morning chill, waitress uniform showing beneath the hem of her
too short coat, scurries toward the coffee shop up the street
where she works. A sturdy, solidly built black woman walks by
dragging a resisting child behind her. A young black man
saunters along slowly as if he has nothing to do and nowhere to
go.

Across the street, a man sits nodding against the iron gate that
protects the entrance to a luggage store. A drug addict. A few
feet away another man has unzipped his pants, starts to urinate
in the street, then changes direction as he tries to catch a passing
car with his stream. Off to the right, toward the corner of Sixth
Avenue, two men stop and hurriedly transact their business. A
buy that will soon send someone else nodding off into a drugged
stupor.

From inside the large apartment building, a steady stream of tenants emerges—middle-class people quite unlike the others with whom they share the street. Some are dressed and looking as if they're ready to meet the day. A few bounce energetically across the lobby in their running clothes. But at this hour, most appear looking fresh from sleep, their clothes flung on carelessly, bare feet stuffed into shoes, as they go out to pick up the morning newspaper or some weekend breakfast treat.

As ten o'clock approaches, the action on the street picks up. The owner of the luggage store, a heavyset Spanish-speaking man, arrives to open it up. He's not gentle with the junkie as he drives him off from the front of his shop. Next door a whole family—mother, father, four children—come to ready a clothing store for business.

The children, too young to be of much help, will try to amuse themselves for the day. But containing their youthful restlessness will be difficult for them. So they'll run in and out all day long, pester their parents for money to buy a hot dog, a taco, a skewer of barbecued meat or one of the other foods the street offers, sometimes fall asleep on a pile of jeans in the middle of the store.

One by one, the iron gates of the shops are pushed aside, bins and racks of merchandise rolled out onto the street, hand-painted placards announcing the bargains of the day strategically placed. Traffic, both foot and vehicular, increases; the tumult escalates; the music shouts its claim for attention; voices are raised as they vie to be heard against the background of noise; puffs of smoke rise from the carts of the food vendors as their cooking begins to coat the neighborhood with its characteristic smells. The street is open for business.

Hawkers stand in front of stores shouting out their bargains. "Check it out! Check it out!" they exhort the passing throngs. Customers stop; the haggling begins. Sometimes a sale is made. More often the negotiation ends with a string of Spanish epithets hurled at the departing back of the customer. Soon the street vendors appear, some selling stolen merchandise, some pushing fraudulent goods—watches with famous names, scarves with cashmere labels, none of them authentic. "Check it out! Check it out!" they cry, as they compete for the attention of the people who pass their way.

This is Bernie Goetz's neighborhood. There are two modern apartment buildings on the stretch of Fourteenth Street between Second and Seventh Avenues, both located between Fifth and Sixth Avenues. Down toward Second Avenue there's some other housing—four-story walk-ups where poor families live. Other than these, the street is home to the Salvation Army, to several unions whose presence in the area pays homage to the days when nearby Union Square was a focal point for union activists, to some large meat-packing plants and to the endless rows of seedy stores with their cheap wares.

No one who lives at 55 West Fourteenth Street would quarrel with the use of the word "unlovely" to describe the neighborhood. At best, the street is a noisy, grimy, ugly place. At worst, it's downright dangerous. The superintendent of Bernie's building tells frightening tales of robberies and muggings that take place daily within sight and sound of the front entrance. Tenants talk of the time when one of the doormen was badly beaten because he tried to move some undesirables away from the front door. The garage attendants say that, in addition to having been robbed at gunpoint themselves, the underground garage has become an escape route for dozens of thieves each week.

And the drug dealers—the ever-present dealers. "I'm constantly being approached by drug dealers as I walk home from the subway," complains one of the tenants in the building. "The other day, from the corner of University Place to Fifth Avenue, I was approached seven times by seven different people. Mind you, these aren't strangers anymore; these are people I see every day. They've become so familiar that I know what type of doughnuts they each eat."

Although there's wide agreement about the problems in the neighborhood, there's no unanimity about the actual dangers on the street. Some tenants who have lived there for years insist they have "never seen a mugging" and "feel perfectly safe on the street because there's always so many people around." At least they did, they say, before Bernie shot his gun.

Now there's an edginess abroad in the building. For some, there's the fear that someone will decide to retaliate against Bernie with a bomb. "Lots of people are afraid; I know I am, or anyway I was a lot when the uproar was so loud. How do we know that some angry black people won't decide they want to get him and leave their calling card in the lobby? Some people have been muttering about wishing he'd move."

Others speak of experiencing an unaccustomed anxiety about their safety in the neighborhood. "I've lived around here forever, and I don't think I ever felt fearful or vulnerable before," says one of his neighbors. "Then one night when I was coming up the subway stairs, there were two black guys behind me. And all of a sudden, I felt scared. I tried to tell myself I was just being nuts, but then I heard a voice behind me saying, 'We're gonna get you Bernie Goetz fans.' Let me tell you, I moved plenty fast to where I knew the cops were stationed near the building."

Hearing these comments about life on Fourteenth Street before Goetz, another resident says angrily, "Well, it's true it's not like Forty-second Street and Eighth Avenue with all that street violence up there. So when they say they've never seen a mugging, maybe they haven't. It's more the general quality of life that people are talking about, and the fact that these dealers and the robbers are an ever-present force in the neighborhood. I don't know where they've been if they don't see that."

"He disliked New York's dirt and crime," Bernie's sister Bernice says after his arrest. Not a surprise, given his background. But if he hated it so much, why did he live on a street where it was so hard to get away from it, a street that is, according to him, "one of the drug centers of New York City"?

The difficulties of New York's housing situation are well known. Apartments are scarce and places in buildings that are little better than slums are expensive. No doubt because the location is such an undesirable one, the tenants in this building on Fourteenth Street get more for their rent money here than in many other places in the city. Yet there surely are other places Bernie could afford that would be more congenial.

For Bernie, however, there seems to be something seductive about the setting. Precisely because of its deficits and discomforts, it provides him with a comprehensible target for the rage that lives inside him. By focusing it on the external world, he need not deal with his internal one. He rails about the dirt, the noise, the drunks, the crime, the pushers, the junkies. And all with good reason. He spends his free time writing letters and petitions, getting signatures, badgering various city agencies and officials to effect the changes he's after. And when he doesn't get action, his anger seems reasonable and just.

No one in the neighborhood likes these things any more than he does; that's what FAB 14th Street, the community cleanup organization, is all about. For others, however, these concerns are but a part of life, a series of tasks to be done to make the neighborhood they live in a little better. For Bernie, these are an obsession, an unyielding, consuming passion that seems to give his life part of its force and energy.

Generally the neighbors agree that the building and the neighborhood make up a good part of Bernie Goetz's life. "The building has always been like a family for him," says one man. "I never could see that he had much of a life outside of it. He doesn't even leave to go to work."

People who support him talk eloquently about how concerned he has always been with the well-being of others. They tell stories about his helpfulness, about how he plays with the children in the lobby, about how he bought a new chair for the doormen to replace an old squeaky one, about the personal money he spent to remove an unsightly placard from the outside of the building.

Others, less approving of his action in shooting the four youths, describe him as obsessed with events in the building and the neighborhood—a moody, unstable man whose life is empty of anything but his work and his activities that center on cleaning up the community.

So, for example, they talk about the time he was agitated about an abandoned newsstand on the corner of Sixth Avenue, an eyesore engorged with trash around which the neighborhood's drug dealers and their customers gathered. For months he petitioned city officials to remove the structure. But his requests went unheeded. One night it burned down. No one knows for sure how it happened, but some people, at least, are convinced that Bernie did it. What everyone agrees on is that he was out on the corner the next day clearing away the debris the fire left.

"A quirky, eccentric guy," concludes one neighbor in a typical comment.

"He doesn't just walk, he rushes around," says another. "He's so tense and withdrawn, you can't really have a normal conversation with him. And when you try, all he can talk about are the neighborhood problems."

In a more compassionate tone, Myra Friedman writes in her *New York* magazine article: "With all his passion for the neighborhood, he somehow remained a loner, a community-minded man uncomfortable with community."

25· The response to the findings of the grand jury is electric. In Barry Slotnick's office, where Bernie Goetz and his defense team get the news, there's a quiet moment of stunned silence. They had hoped for it, but nobody expected it. Then a joyful pandemonium takes over. "We danced and had a drink and congratulated ourselves," recalls Slotnick. "After a while, Bernie asked me, 'What do I do now?' and I said, 'Leave town!'" Advice given only half in jest, and which Bernie and his lawyers would soon wish he had taken more seriously.

Elsewhere questions fly thick and fast. It's common knowledge that a grand jury usually is the playground of the prosecutor. In the world of criminal law, the rare grand jury that defies the district attorney's recommendations is called a "runaway grand jury." What happened in this grand jury room? people are now asking. What evidence could have been presented to convince the jurors that Bernie Goetz was justified in shooting all four youths? What instructions did the prosecutor give them? Only a majority vote is necessary to hand up an indictment. How close was the vote?

Even many Goetz supporters are bemused by this turn of events. They're happy he won't have to face a trial for attempted murder. But it's all so unexpected that it's hard to integrate.

. . .

After the fact as well as during the proceedings, the secrecy of the grand jury is inviolate. When first impaneled, jurors are sworn not to disclose anything about the business of the grand jury. To protect them from public pressure and inquiry, their identity is never revealed.

Witnesses before a New York grand jury are not permitted to have an attorney present unless they have waived immunity. Only then is a defense attorney allowed inside the room during a client's testimony. And although the attorney and client may confer in this instance, the attorney may not speak or question the client before the jurors.

The only official source of information after a case is heard, therefore, is the district attorney. And he, too, is constrained by law from discussing who the witnesses were, what they said, what he presented to the jurors or how he presented it.

Legally no one can keep witnesses or their attorneys from speaking out. But since defense attorneys usually are not permitted to accompany clients into the jury room, they generally can say nothing from firsthand observation. And so far in this case, there has been silence from those who were witnesses.

Immediately after the grand jurors come to their decision, Morgenthau holds a press conference. After viewing the videotape and hearing from more than a dozen witnesses, he now tells the world, the jurors were asked to consider indictments on four counts of attempted murder, four of assault, four of reckless endangerment and one count of criminal possession of a weapon, the last a more serious charge than the ones on which Goetz was indicted.

They deliberated for seventy minutes before reaching their verdict, the DA reveals, a decision that relied on the law of justification which permits a person to use deadly force to defend himself if he reasonably believes he is about to be hurt, killed or robbed. "This grand jury believed he used reasonable force," Morgenthau asserts. "They heard all the facts and they did not believe he committed a crime in the shootings."

Asked how he thinks the public might interpret the grand jury's action, the district attorney says, "I hope what they read is that, in this specific case, the grand jury found there was justification. I hope they won't read anything more into it. I also hope they notice he was indicted for a felony and faces up to seven years in prison."

Thirty minutes later, Joseph Kelner holds his own news conference and tells the world that, in his view, the grand jury's action is "practically an exoneration of our client." Mayor Koch, talking to reporters at City Hall at about the same time, acclaims the verdict as "Solomonic." And Roy Innis, national chairman of the Congress of Racial Equality, praises the decision as a "reaffirmation of the fundamental right of self-defense." Even Governor Cuomo, appearing on WNBC-TV's *Live at 5*, refuses to question the jurors' decision. "You don't know what the grand jury was told," he says. "Why should we assume they acted irresponsibly? I'm going to believe they acted responsibly."

Howard Meyer, attorney for Troy Canty, is shocked. "He shot four kids . . . two of them in the back. What kind of a hero is that? He's white, and the four kids he shot were black. It's absurd to think he didn't intend to murder them." Ronald Kuby, who represents Shirley Cabey, announces that she is "in shock" and issues a statement on her behalf. "She said that what the government is now telling people is that it is all right to go out and pick up guns and shoot black people."

From Concord, New Hampshire, Police Chief Walchak says, "It's like everything else; most of the time the system works; sometimes it doesn't. And from what I know of the Goetz case, the system didn't work. I don't know all the evidence the grand jury got, of course, but if there wasn't anything but the evidence we gave them, it was more than enough to indict. It's not for the grand jurors to judge whether he's guilty or innocent. They only need to decide whether a possible crime was committed."

The questions about the case, about how the DA handled it, about what he did or didn't say to the jurors, don't go away. Morgenthau responds defensively. He presented all the available evidence, did all he could, he insists. He didn't try to move the panel toward any particular indictment because that's not his policy. "We don't ever push a grand jury to return an indictment," he asserts. . . . "We give them the facts and the law and we let them make up their minds. We leave it to them."

To which Richard Emery, a staff attorney for the New York Civil Liberties Union, responds angrily. Grand juries "are notoriously subject to a prosecutor's objectives. . . . There is no opposition during the grand jury presentation to what the prosecutor is saying. Therefore, they generally follow what the prosecutor wants."

In an article on the New York *Times*'s Op Ed page a few days later, Emery challenges the basis for secrecy in grand jury proceedings. In this case in particular, he argues, it was pointless, not in the public interest and "nurturing [of] an atmosphere in which cynicism about the criminal justice system and accusations of racial bias flourished.

"Did the prosecutor . . . give in to public pressure to exonerate Mr. Goetz?" he asks. "Why did the prosecutor refuse to call even one of the four young men who were shot, when apparently none of them is to be charged? What did the prosecutor's assistant mean by stating at the public arraignment that there was no justification for the shootings? She knew the evidence. How could the grand jury disagree? Because of grand jury secrecy, these questions will never be answered."

A few days later, Martin Garbus, a criminal lawyer in New

York, writes on the same Op Ed page of the *Times*: "District Attorney Robert M. Morgenthau's statement about the jurors—'We gave them the facts and the law and we let them make up their minds'—is disingenuous in the extreme. . . . [His] claim that he does not press for indictments before any grand juries is also nonsense. So is the assertion that he does not guide or direct the grand juries under his supervision. He does it in nearly every case. That is precisely what he was elected to do."

Alan Dershowitz, nationally renowned criminal lawyer and professor of law at Harvard University, also enters the fray. "Every experienced criminal lawyer understands that grand jurors rarely act on their own," he writes. "They generally do the bidding of the prosecutor 'in charge' of the grand jury. . . . I have been told many times by prosecutors that unless a suspect cooperates, 'I [the prosecutor] will have my grand jury indict him in five minutes.'

"It's almost unheard-of for a grand jury to refuse to follow the 'recommendations' of its prosecutor. . . . The prosecutor controls the grand jury in subtle as well as overt ways. The evidence presented, the tone of voice, the nature of the legal instructions—these may be more important than any overt recommendation."

The debate about whether Morgenthau should have given immunity to any of the victims of the shootings also heats up again. Angrily, Howard Meyer recalls the way the prosecutor brought the youths into the grand jury room knowing they would refuse to testify without immunity. "If they had wanted to set them up, they couldn't have done it better. You know what people think when they hear someone take the Fifth Amendment. They've all heard racketeers and gangsters and the like take the Fifth. What kind of impact could it have had on the grand jury to call each of them in just so they could refuse to sign a waiver of immunity?

"You'll notice," he continues, "they didn't make Goetz go

through the same routine and take the Fifth. If they had, at least the grand jurors would have seen that both sides weren't going to testify without immunity. As it was, only the kids were seen pleading the Fifth."

Other attorneys experienced in criminal law agree, insisting that Morgenthau's decisions were based on political considerations, not legal ones. He already knew that there probably would be no charges arising from this case against these young men, they say. In fact, early on he said publicly that there was no evidence against them. But even if there was some doubt about that, these experts argue, why couldn't he have given immunity to only one of the four? Based on what he knew from Goetz's confession about the events on that subway, he could surely have chosen the one who seemed least culpable of any untoward activity that day. Without such testimony, the grand jurors heard only Bernie Goetz's side of the story.

In a blistering and caustic attack on the credibility of the district attorney's actions in the case, Professor Dershowitz dubs the DA a "vigilante prosecutor." "There is one phenomenon even more dangerous than a vigilante subway shooter," he writes. "That is a vigilante prosecutor who takes the law into his own political hands, while pretending that the decision was made exclusively by an independent grand jury."

On the surface, Morgenthau seems unmoved by the charges against him. But there are signs to indicate that the strain is beginning to tell. Although he continues to stand by his original decisions in the case, including his refusal to give immunity to any of the youths, his explanations become more frequent and more insistent. He speaks repeatedly about the risks entailed in the automatic immunity New York's law confers—from the possibility that a criminal will "bathe himself in immunity" and become invulnerable to prosecution for some serious crime, to the chance that the jury will react against the deal. "That's what immunity is—a deal," he asserts. "And when you go to trial, the defense beats you over the head with it."

He reminds people, also, that since Goetz had already admitted he shot the youths, the case against him was strong enough without bringing them before a grand jury. But if this was true, why did he subpoena them? What was to be gained by forcing them to refuse to waive immunity in the presence of the grand jury? Surely he must have known that this could only leave the jurors more suspicious of the youths than they already were.

To these questions, there are no easy answers. There's little doubt that Mr. Morgenthau is an honest, able and respected prosecutor. But to believe that any elected official in this nation, including a district attorney, makes decisions based on the law alone, without regard for the political context, is naïve in the extreme.

Ten years as Manhattan's district attorney and before that nine years as the United States Attorney in New York's Southern District have given Morgenthau plenty of practice in juggling the often conflicting pressures of political necessity, public opinion, interest-group pressure and the law. During most of the month of January when the negotiations around immunity were going on, he was undoubtedly seeking an outcome in the case that would relieve him of looking like the hoodlums' savior and the hero's executioner.

Now, as the days pass and the pressure of criticism mounts, he begins to back away from what earlier seemed to be his easy and approving acceptance of the grand jury's decision. Now he shakes his head in wonder as he says, "The jury really bought the justification argument, I suppose, but they were also expressing their views about subway crime. Here we had a man where the evidence shows he shot two people in the back and where his own statements were extremely damaging. It didn't seem possible they wouldn't indict him."

26 · In keeping with the notion that the less the accused says, the better, until now Bernie Goetz has heeded his lawyer's advice and kept out of sight. His friends say he's been complaining about being stuck in his apartment. He wants "to walk on the street and be back in public again," they tell the press. Now that the grand jury's verdict is in, he gets his wish.

But much to the surprise of Goetz watchers, the man who comes out of seclusion is very different from the one who went into it. In the next few weeks, the shy, retiring man who wanted anonymity just a month ago moves into the limelight as if he were born to it, unable, it seems, to pull himself away from the public gaze. The caterpillar has been transformed into a butterfly.

Even his friend Tom Stotler is perplexed as he watches Bernie from the quiet of his New Hampshire bookstore. "It looks like he's gotten carried away," he says. "I think he has now moved into a sort of martyr role. He sees himself as a martyr who challenged the system and said to the lawyers and police and judges: If you're not going to do the job, I'll create an incident that will put you on the hot seat. He doesn't think he did anything wrong. He did what had to be done, and he's glad he did it. He's not all wrong, but he's a little wacky."

Each day the press reports a new escapade. He rides the subways without any particular destination, accepting the applause and congratulations of other passengers with a warm smile. He talks to them about the need for self-protection, about his belief, now becoming a cause for him, that New York's gun-licensing law must be revised.

A young black man tells of running into Bernie on the downtown Seventh Avenue express late one Friday night, close to midnight. He's thought a good deal about Bernie Goetz and the four youths he shot. The grand jury's verdict a couple of weeks ago seemed to him to be an invitation to more bloody confrontations between white men and black ones. He's been wary ever since it came down that way.

But he isn't thinking of any of this as he enters the subway car and settles himself on a bench. It's the music he just heard that preoccupies his thoughts, that and the somewhat overheated ride that lies ahead. Until he looks up to see Bernie Goetz sitting a few feet away.

Startled, he's flooded once again with the anger he's known since the shootings first occurred. He sits perfectly still in his seat, staring at Bernie, daring him to look in his direction. "Christ," he says to himself, "it's hard to believe that this guy's just riding around as if nothing happened."

He watches Bernie smile as he talks to a man and woman nearby. "Thanks," he hears him say as the man offers congratulations on his grand jury victory. "No," Bernie replies to a question asked too quietly to be overheard. "They're not going to make me leave the city. I'm going to stay and fight. We all have to fight and keep pressuring these people who are running things and letting the criminals take over the city."

The black man listens and simmers, until someone shouts out, "Hey, Bernie, whaddya doin' ridin' the train?" That breaks the tension for him, and he laughs. But Bernie turns toward the questioner and replies seriously, "Well, you know, there's been a lot of shit in the papers about me lately, and I'm here to counteract it. It's a dirty game, and I hate playing it, but what else can I do? I have to be out here meeting the people and letting them know the truth." With that, he stands up and in a voice loud enough to be heard throughout most of the car: "There are probably two or three people carrying guns on this car right now. What else can any of us do in this city?"

The man telling the story shudders as he recalls Bernie's words. "This guy's not just some kook," he says, "he's dangerous. He's running around town advocating that people arm themselves. What the hell will happen if they take his advice? There'll be some kind of a bloodbath going on out there."

By way of explaining his client's sudden visibility, Kelner announces to the press that Bernie has a "strong desire" to focus national attention "into obtaining a betterment of security for the public. . . . He would like to see a shake-up in our criminal justice procedures so there is a stronger control over crime and what it is doing to cause all of us to live in fear."

Even if wholly true, however, as an explanation it's only a partial one. For transformations such as we're witness to in Bernie are not born of anything quite so rational. Certainly our experiences in the world shape who we are and what we become. They help us to change and grow, to cast aside old ways of being and take on new ones. Of course, ideas and beliefs influence how we behave. But *how* that influence will be expressed, how external events impact upon our internal world and are then translated into behavior, depends upon a complex mélange of past experience and our own unique synthetic capabilities.

Inside all of us lives our opposite, sometimes quite well developed, sometimes not. Either way, the face we show to the world lives side by side with its hidden contradiction. The blustering blowhard hides the frightened and insecure part of the self; the timid socially retarded part obscures from public view the grandiose one.

We may not know *why* these opposing selves exist inside us. But most of the time, we're quite conscious of the presence of this shadow side, even take some comfort in it in the privacy of our inner life. Like Walter Mitty, who became a folk hero precisely because he tapped a reality that lives beyond the confines of the tale that gave him life, we, too, turn inward to allow ourselves feelings and impulses forbidden elsewhere, to bring our fantasies to life.

So it is with Bernie as well. For him, it seems clear that it was his internal grandiose self that salved the distress of the external timid one. Psychologists know that the kind of contempt he shows for authority, for those who disagree with his vision of the world, the certainty he displays in the face of the complex issues he speaks of, generally are expressions of a grandiose self. Until now, this side had been kept in check by his place in the world. When that place changed, as it has over these recent weeks, the grandiose side could come out of hiding.

The emergence of the myth of Bernie-as-folk-hero, as national savior, gave permission to his grandiosity and validated this sense of himself that for so long had been kept under wraps. Now, finally, the world could recognize what, in one part of himself, he had believed all along—that he's better and smarter than the people around him, that their failure to appreciate him until now was their shortcoming, not his.

But this doesn't mean the shy and timid Bernie is just a fake, a cover for the grandiose one. No, both are real—part of the contradictions that live inside him. The face he has presented to the world until now is still there, still comes to the fore to compete with the new one that seems to be emerging so forcefully at the moment. While one side is on stage, the other is in the wings, waiting for the cues that will call it forth. This is why he seems so hard to figure out, why at one moment he's such a sympathetic figure and at another seems so abrasive.

Wherever Bernie goes, of course, the press is sure to follow. More and more, he becomes the embodiment of the myth the press and public have created. The act has come to define the man. He who so recently cringed at being called a hero, who hated the labels the media pinned on him, seems now to have come to believe them.

Every day, his views on crime in the streets and how to combat it are published in the papers, reported on television and radio. "You've got to teach them how to get the gun out quickly," he tells an audience. "You can't have a guy fumbling with the weapon, trying to get it out of his pocket and dropping it. Crimes happen too quickly for that."

It's not just his concern for crime that motivates such public statements, however. Rather, it would seem that Bernie also wants others to do what he did, partly because it will give legitimacy to his own act, and partly because their emulation will make their admiration more real.

Every day, new pictures appear showing his movements about the city. Amid TV cameras and flashing strobes, he attends the funeral of a seventy-one-year-old former Harlem school principal who was shot to death in a robbery, making his usual statements about the ineptitude of the criminal justice system along the way. Embarrassingly, the expected open-armed greeting doesn't materialize. Instead, the family and friends of the dead man make it clear he's not welcome there.

A black factory worker named Andrew Frederick tries to stop someone from stealing candy from a subway newsstand and, in the scuffle that ensues, stabs the thief to death. Uninvited, Bernie Goetz appears at the arraignment proceedings, press and TV cameras trailing in his wake. "Mr. Frederick reprimanded them for what only can be considered socially unacceptable conduct," Bernie announces. "Their reaction should have been one of shame." In a television interview later in the day, he stands with

Frederick and tells the public, "We need more of this," and asks people to "relate to this man." Andrew Frederick, a man who apparently has deep regrets over the stabbing that brought Bernie rushing to his side, looks distinctly uncomfortable.

Bernie now gives interviews fairly freely, especially to the paper he can count on for unquestioning loyalty, the New York *Post*. And in what appears to be a well-orchestrated public relations campaign, the people around him, who formerly were enjoined from making any public statements at all, are now available for questions and comments.

Bernard Goldstein, one of his electronics buddies who is co-chair of the Goetz Legal Defense Fund, tells the press that Bernie was accosted by muggers before, in an incident on 110th Street near Harlem. He pulled a gun that time, too, Goldstein says, but he didn't shoot. "It shows," says Goldstein, "he's not an irresponsible man—he didn't just shoot unless he had to."

As they continue to build the portrait of Bernie as a caring, responsible, self-sacrificing citizen, Joseph Kelner recounts for the press two instances when his client came to the aid of women being mugged—one on Park Avenue somewhere around Fiftieth Street, the other near the boathouse in Central Park. It's not long before one of the women he allegedly helped tells the press she never heard of him until he became headline news and doesn't know what he's talking about. Her purse was snatched in Central Park all right, she says, but Bernie Goetz was nowhere in sight when it happened.

27· With the grand jury's virtual exoneration of Bernie, black and white opinion begins to separate. For the first time, New York City's Police Commissioner Benjamin Ward, a black man, makes a public statement saying that Bernie Goetz should have been indicted "for some level of assault, right up to possible attempted murder. . . . You don't shoot two people in the back when they're running away from you and say it's self-defense."

Black activists, convinced that the grand jury's decision was motivated by racism, ask for a prosecution under federal civil rights law. United States Attorney Rudolph Giuliani says he'll be happy to meet with the people calling for a federal investigation of the case, but warns against any expectations that he will find a basis for federal action.

Kelner quickly announces that these minority leaders are taking "an unfortunate path. . . . There is no racism here and there is no violation of civil rights. . . . This is not a man who is antiblack. . . . He is color-blind so far as blacks and whites are concerned."

"Color-blind!" scoffs one of Bernie's neighbors, recalling the times he and others heard him make racist statements either privately or publicly at the meetings of FAB 14th Street. "I can't remember the exact things he said, but color-blind he isn't, of that I assure you." But Myra Friedman remembers, as her *New York* magazine article tells. There she recounts her shock at hearing Bernie say, "The only way we're going to clean up this street is to get rid of the spics and niggers." A remark that so stunned the assembled group that, for a time, he wasn't permitted to join it.

When these charges are made public, some of Bernie's champions cry foul and insist he could never have said such a thing. But Bernie himself doesn't deny it, as he would tell a reporter some time later. "Five or six years ago, I was asked not to join one association that was being formed because of racial comments I made. By the way, I've used the word 'nigger' or 'spic' since then."

Other supporters explain that he was just kidding around, that he didn't mean anything when he made such remarks. "That's just the way people talk," says one man dismissively. "Bernie says things like that sometimes just to shake people up, but he's no racist. Those people are just looking to make trouble for him," he complains indignantly.

Undoubtedly this is the way some people talk. But the explanation is hardly a defense against the racist charge. In any case, a look at his confession to the Concord police is enough to make any reasonable observer doubt the color-blind label. There it's obvious that he was quite aware of the color of the young men from the moment he walked into the subway car. And when he stopped shooting and walked through the train to see that everyone else was all right, he noticed the color of the two women he thought he might have injured, describing them to the police quite graphically as a middle-aged black woman and a white blonde.

Finally, months later, he's still making comments and observations to suggest he's neither color-blind nor without prejudice. Rather, as is true of so many white Americans, he has mixed feelings and thoughts on the subject of race. Thus in one moment, he tells of warning a friend who has used the word "niggers," "You've got to judge them as individuals. Some are as fine people as you want to meet; some are the scum of the earth." But when asked if this isn't true of all groups, he replies, as if he hadn't uttered the caution against racial generalizations a moment ago, "It's more extreme with black people. . . . The society has dishonesty and lies at all levels. . . . [But] lying and dishonesty in the black community is more pronounced."

On February 6, Bernie appears in a Manhattan courtroom once again, this time to plead not guilty to the gun charges now lodged against him. Until now, only well-wishers greeted his public appearances. Now, for the first time, there are protesters outside the courtroom—a small group of about forty demonstrators, black and white, who shout angrily about "racist violence."

Inside, except for a few whispered words with his lawyers, Bernie is silent throughout the brief fifteen-minute hearing. The judge, saying there's a "stark contrast" between the original charges and the weapons possession charges for which he will be tried, reduces bail from $50,000 to $5,000. Still cautious, however, he also orders Bernie to surrender his passport.

After weeks of speculation about the content of Myra Friedman's tapes, her article, which is little more than an edited version of her conversations with Bernie, appears under the title "My Neighbor Bernie Goetz." The tapes tell the tale of a frightened, angry, often rambling and incoherent man—a man in struggle as he twists and turns between insistent self-righteousness and deep agitation.

He responded "viciously and savagely," like a rat who was cornered, he told Friedman. Others may say he did "the right thing," he said, but at this early moment in the history of the events that would surround and eventually help shape Bernie Goetz, he refused to join them in this judgment. "I'm not going to say that. I think what I did was appropriate or reasonable, if you can believe that, under the circumstances."

Yet in the next breath, he talked with absolute certainty about the correctness of his act, expressed outrage about those who thought his behavior was "crazy" or "uncivilized." "Can you believe that, Myra! I heard some attorney from the Civil Liberties Union on television yesterday saying that I responded in an uncivilized way."

In the kind of quick shift that characterized these conversations, he put away his doubts, insisted upon the necessity of his behavior, raged at the legal system, which he called "a farce" and "a self-serving bureaucracy," mocked the lawyers "who want to defend me for free." Lawyers whose offers he would soon accept happily.

No matter what aspect of the shootings Bernie and Friedman discussed, the turmoil inside him, the conflicting and contradictory thoughts, were apparent. She asked him if, before the shootings of December 22, he had thought he might get angry enough to do such a thing. He accused her of not understanding. Of course "there is a type of premeditation to your thinking," he granted, if you plan to defend yourself with a weapon. But he didn't plan the shootings before he boarded the train, he assured her.

Pleading with her to grasp what he was trying to say, he cried, "See, Myra, you don't understand the situation in New York. . . . The people *have* to have guns. And yet the city tells you, 'Don't you *dare* have a gun; you get a one-year mandatory.' I mean, this is just for starters. See, Myra, you don't understand."

In their first conversation, he talked about coming back to New York and forgetting the whole thing, just living as if it didn't happen. But if he ever seriously believed he could carry out such a plan, he found out differently when he returned to his apartment the next day and learned he was wanted for questioning by the police.

In the second conversation, made the next day, he said sadly, "Myra, what I did—I turned into a monster, and that's the truth." As in their earlier conversation, the issue of his privacy was in the forefront of his mind, as he talked about his plan to turn himself in. He wanted only to be left alone, to live quietly, to return to the anonymity that had been his protection and the hallmark of his life until this time. He would tell the police everything they wanted to know, didn't care what they would do with or to him, he said, if they would only "give me my privacy."

But if all he wanted was anonymity and privacy, why did Bernie Goetz call Myra Friedman, a woman who says, "I hardly knew him"? Sure, she had seen him in the elevator or in the lobby of their building often enough. He'd be hard to miss, as many of his neighbors would attest. "I've lived in this building for six years," says a man who himself isn't around very much, "and from day one Bernie was a visible figure. He was a presence you couldn't miss in the day-to-day trafficking coming in and out of the building." For those like Myra Friedman, who either work at home or don't have regular nine-to-five jobs, he was, in her words, "an omnipresent person. You almost couldn't get on the elevator without finding him there."

There are others who live in the building who now say they're friends of Bernie, even some who call themselves "good" friends. Yet he contacted this woman who says she's a relative stranger to him instead of one of these people.

Partly perhaps that's because these friendships have blossomed largely in the aftermath of the shootings. And as is so often our wont, the people involved have rewritten their history to serve the needs of the moment. Before this, they were neighbors. They saw each other around the building, perhaps appreciated Bernie's

often frenzied activities on behalf of the community organization that sought to make Fourteenth Street a safer, better place
to live. But all the evidence suggests that they were not friends
in the sense that they shared either lives or thoughts.

One neighbor, speaking about these people who now claim
such close friendship with Bernie, says scornfully, "Nobody
can deny it. There was an air of excitement in the building, and
some people tried very hard to secure their positions. They
were not very graceful about it. You'd see them lurking in the
lobbies just waiting for the TV crews to turn their attention to
them. Some of them who suddenly became Bernie's good friends
put on a really revolting display. It makes you think in terms
of Warhol's concept of fifteen minutes of fame."

But perhaps also it's not coincidental that Bernie Goetz chose
to call a writer rather than one of the other neighbors in his
building. Perhaps he wanted her to write the story—to write
it as only he would tell it. Why else did he ask her to come to
Connecticut with "a couple of the Guardian Angels and a tape
recorder"?

Reflecting on these questions, a longtime resident of the
building comments, "I wouldn't underestimate his pathology any
more than I would underestimate his cunning." And Friedman
herself says, "I don't know why he called me. I asked him that,
and he didn't answer. But there was no foundation in reality for
him to have called me as a friend or even as a friendly neighbor.
I wasn't.

"On the other hand, he had seen me around the building, and
maybe in his mind I seemed to project some kind of sympathetic
quality. Along with that was his awareness that I was a journalist.
I suspect he was ambivalent about it, but he was the one who
first brought up writing, not me.

"I myself don't believe there was one single motive for the
call, but rather a myriad of motives, some of which may forever
remain in the strange dark shadows of the utterly bizarre. But
the fact that I was a writer could not have been far from con-

sciousness. Nor does it look like he called me on snap impulse either. The shooting happened on December 22; he called me on the 29th. In other words, he had a week to think it over."

For the first time, the Friedman tapes also reveal that, during the Vietnam War, Bernie Goetz was classified 4-F on the basis of psychiatric disability. "I did everything I could to get out of Vietnam, and I did," he bragged to Friedman in response to her question about why he hadn't been in the army. "In terms of beating the system and stuff like that, I beat it good. . . . A psychiatrist trained me to act like a complete psychotic."

Certainly he "beat the system." But it doesn't take a highly trained clinical person to conclude that the so-called training he received fell on fertile ground. There's nothing at all to suggest that Bernie Goetz is actually psychotic. But there's little doubt that this is a man whose personality features some distinctly, and probably dangerous, paranoid characteristics.

His lifelong isolation has left him without the resources for the kind of external reality checks most of us take for granted. People who are close to others turn to them in moments of stress and doubt to check out the meaning of an event or an interaction. Here's what happened, and here's what was said, we'll tell a friend. What do you think it means? we'll ask. Did I interpret it correctly? Did I do something wrong? Did he really mean to hurt me?

Without this kind of feedback, we're wholly dependent, as Bernie Goetz has been for the whole of his life until now, on our own internal dialogue. Without it, we all can get lost in the quagmire of our own thoughts and feelings, of distorted perceptions that have little relationship to reality, of fears that are projections of our own internal states.

28. As Bernie becomes more visible and more vocal in the month following the grand jury's verdict, public adoration, or at least the noisy demonstration and articulation of it, begins to erode. It's as if the more they see, the less they like. Even people who have been solidly in his corner begin to express doubts.

Typically, we Americans look warily at ideologues; we don't appreciate people who take themselves so seriously. So the private man—the shy, quiet loner who, when he was minding his own business, got caught in a web that was not of his making—is more to our liking than this public figure with his personal ax to grind. Reflecting on this turn of events, the tough New Hampshireman Tom Stotler says with a rueful smile, "I said to him just a little while ago, you know, Bernie, your mouth is going to get you in more trouble than your gun."

The emerging Bernie, so different from the one people thought they knew and understood, helps to keep questions about him, about the case itself, alive. Many Americans, in and out of New York, found that the grand jury's verdict left a sour taste in their mouths, a sense of unease and discomfort that would not go away. Now their doubts escalate. It's not that these people want to convict Bernie Goetz, but there's a feeling abroad that there should have been a trial. At least, they're saying, that would clear the air, put the questions to rest once and for all.

Whatever he may have thought or done during the grand jury proceedings originally, District Attorney Morgenthau is responsive to the newly developing climate, perhaps even helps to build it. The press reports that prosecutors are looking into the possibility of another weapons charge against Goetz—this time for the sale of guns. Morgenthau confirms the report, saying if there's sufficient evidence, the matter will be turned over to the grand jury.

At the same time, there are persistent rumors that he's seeking new evidence in the hope of reopening the original case. In a move that signals an aggressive new stance, Susan Braver is relieved and Gregory Waples, reputed to be the best and toughest prosecutor in the DA's office, is assigned to the case.

While all this is in the air, Darrell Cabey's lawyers file a $50 million civil suit in Bronx Supreme Court alleging that he was shot in the back "deliberately, willfully and with malice" as he "attempted to flee." A few days later, another suit is filed, this time on behalf of Troy Canty. The action, filed in Manhattan Supreme Court, charges Goetz with assault and battery and asks $5 million in damages.

On the next-to-the-last day of February, Bernie Goetz is in court once again, this time for a procedural hearing in connection with his indictment on the gun charges. From the beginning, Bernie's attorneys have requested that they be permitted to see the Concord police reports and the taped confession in order to prepare their defense. Until now, the DA has objected, maintaining that since they are part of the evidence presented to the grand jury, they must remain secret. Now the prosecutor unexpectedly withdraws his objection and turns over to the court the documents the defense has been requesting, a move that transforms these secret documents into public ones.

Both sides are reminded by Manhattan's Supreme Court Justice Stephen Crane, who has been hearing motions in the case, that the Code of Professional Responsibility forbids the disclosure of the contents of any admission or statement made by the accused. Since the tapes fall into the category of an admission, they are enjoined from making them public. The defense requests that the police reports—that is, the written statements of the officers who took Goetz's statement—be sealed as well. But the prosecution objects. Morgenthau later explains, "We thought the statements should be before the public." The judge rules for the prosecution, and the police reports are placed in the court record, thereby becoming public documents.

Reporters rush to examine the newly released evidence, their eagerness fed by the search for a scoop, by the wish to be the first to tell the world of some startling new revelation. Barring that, they hope at least they'll find a new angle in this story that has by now become so old. Within hours, their wishes come true. The headlines herald their front-page stories: "Goetz Admits Taking Second Shot at Teen," "Goetz Shocker: I Shot Him Again," "Goetz Told Victim: 'Here's Another'—and Fired Again."

For the first time, the public hears in a way that cannot be ignored that after he shot the youths, Bernhard Goetz calmly checked the condition of each one to, in his own words, "make sure they were cold, that they'd been taken care of." Three of the four were lying on the floor, blood from their wounds clearly visible. The fourth, Darrell Cabey, was still, as Bernie himself told it, "half sitting, half lying on the bench where he was originally." He apparently had never moved from his seat except to stand up and look away, pretending he wasn't with the others, according to Goetz's own version of the story. After looking Darrell over and seeing no blood, Bernie told the police that he said to him, "You seem to be doing all right, here's another," and shot him again—a shot that turned Darrell Cabey into a cripple, both physically and mentally, for the rest of his life.

For the first time, too, the press and public get the full flavor of Bernie's self-righteousness. He knew what he did was cold-blooded, he told the police, but he didn't feel it was wrong. Not wrong to shoot two people in the back? To go back for a second shot? a reporter asks him some time later. "Under the circumstances, shooting in the back is irrelevant," he replies. Does he mean defensible? No. "Irrelevant," he insists, and tells a story he seems to think is a metaphor for his own: A woman who has been raped sees the man who did it coming toward her on the street one day. She stabs him forty-two times. "Was the thirty-fifth stab self-defense? Was the twentieth self-defense?" he asks. "And shooting people in the back; is that self-defense?"

It's not a conversation; he doesn't wait for a response, doesn't really seem to want one. He already knows what the answer should be, and that's what counts. If "the system" wouldn't take care of such things, someone had to. "Somebody has to stand for something," he tells the *Post* in another interview following the release of the police reports, "and I stood for something."

People are shaken by the facts that are now being put so forcefully before them. For the moment, at least, the Goetz bandwagon is substantially slowed. Opponents now call more vigorously than ever for some new attempt at prosecuting him. The press, until now cautious about tangling with the dominant, or at least the noisiest, sector of public opinion about Bernie Goetz, changes its tune.

On their editorial pages, both the New York *Daily News* and the *Times* recount the events, take Morgenthau seriously to task for his role in the grand jury's verdict, and demand that he take the case back to a second grand jury and try again. "Is a man who methodically shoots four possibly threatening human beings, two in the back and then, according to a police statement, shoots one of them a second time because he doesn't see blood, guilty?" asks the *News*.

"That's debatable," the editorial continues, but such "important questions of guilt and innocence [must] be decided publicly, under rules and procedures that make sense, that are accountable. . . . The case *can* go back to the grand jury, with judicial approval. It should. It must."

The *Times*, too, asks indignantly, "How can such calculated vengeance possibly be explained as self-defense? And how could a grand jury, which heard all these details, have indicted only for illegal gun possession? Did District Attorney Robert Morgenthau do all he could to secure indictment for the tougher charges?

"The Manhattan prosecutors say . . . they were astounded at the outcome. Astonishment isn't enough. The Goetz case raises profound public questions, which the public is left to debate on the basis of spotty information. They can only be properly laid to rest in a trial."

Supporters are divided. Some insist that nothing has changed. The fact is, they say, he was accosted by four punks and he shot them. How he did it, or what he did after that, is of no consequence. "Don't tell me I'm supposed to feel sorry for those animals," snaps a bartender angrily. "Those mothers deserve whatever Bernie gave them. It's about time someone put the fear of God into them. I don't give a damn about any of this stuff they're talking about now. As far as I'm concerned, more power to him. When he shot that gun, he was shooting for all of us."

In a more measured statement, Herbert London, dean of the Gallatin Division of New York University, writes: "Perhaps the Goetz response to the actions of his accosters was not entirely warranted—a point that has not yet been determined. Nonetheless, who can sit in judgment of someone who resists a shakedown? . . . For New Yorkers who are obliged to ride the trains and for those who have had the misfortune to be mugged, they will not retreat from defending Bernhard Goetz. He may not be all that we might like in a defender of law and order, but then again, there are very few New Yorkers who have not been cowed by the street thugs and revolving door justice."

But others are less certain. Shaking his head doubtfully, one of Bernie's former schoolmates says, "I couldn't shoot anybody myself, leastways I don't think I could, but I could sure appreciate his feelings about those people and what he did. Or at least I could until this new information that's been released lately. Now I figure that maybe it wasn't just what happened in the subway that day. Maybe things were just building up in him so much and he finally blew.

"You know, when it first occurred, I thought it was a self-defense kind of thing. But now it doesn't seem so clear anymore. It seems to me there might be something more to it—something psychological, like something else happened inside him. But who am I to say anything about that?"

Mayor Koch, who has been on all sides of this case, has no such reservations about speaking out once again. Instead, he announces that he's going to "take a step back" from the whole mess. Bernie's proposal that more New Yorkers be allowed to carry guns, he says, is "Looneyville," and these new revelations suggest that he may be "a flake." No, he now declares, he has no objections to a new grand jury inquiry.

And Governor Cuomo says that although he doesn't know what difference it will make legally, he believes the news that Bernie fired a second shot at a person who was already defenseless "is a significant fact."

Robert Morgenthau, a man people call a consummate politician, surely was aware of what he would stir up when he insisted upon making the police reports public. Clearly by then he was having second thoughts about the first grand jury's decision. And although he continues to deny that any political concerns motivated him, then or now, his disclaimers don't match his behavior, then or now.

In January there was no indication that he had any quarrel with the grand jury's verdict. Or at least none he was willing to make public. Then, he said he believed the grand jurors had been "conscientious," that they had done a thoughtful job. Now, he says he was shocked by their decision and has been "considering re-presenting [the case to a new grand jury] from the day the indictment was voted. . . . But just because a prosecutor is not happy over a grand jury action is not a basis for re-presenting. . . . I've got to have a substantial basis for doing it."

But there's little doubt that in addition to the "substantial basis," he also needed and wanted public backing. Did he engineer the release of these damaging documents in his quest for support for a new grand jury inquiry? He smiles enigmatically when the question is asked, and says, "I'm certainly responsible for making them public."

29. Under New York State law, a case may be resubmitted to a second grand jury only if there is new evidence or grounds for additional charges. In the Goetz case, the DA says, if Darrell Cabey dies, there could well be additional charges to present. If he recovers and agrees to testify without immunity, or if any one of the other youths can be persuaded to do so, it might constitute new evidence. Word is out that one of them has already been contacted by the district attorney's office.

A worried Kelner points out that nothing new has been revealed, since the first grand jury already had all the information that now seems to be causing such consternation. Barry Slotnick denounces those who would reopen the case, accusing "various fringe elements" of attempting to undermine the grand jury's action. "It's unfortunate that there has been immense pressure put upon those in the criminal justice system by individuals who have a vested interest in attacking Bernhard Goetz."

But his words have a hollow ring, since a matching concern for the integrity of the criminal justice system was absent when the pressure was all in favor of his client. And the "fringe elements" he refers to include the governor, the district attorney, dozens of well-respected members of the bar, the New York *Times* and the *Daily News*.

Bernie Goetz responds as well. New York is "sick from one end to another," he says angrily. But he's not worried about these attempts to send the case before another grand jury, he tells the press. "Sure, they're looking for one little thing to condemn me, but the truth will all come out eventually. Once again, I'm back to being cornered like a rat. Now suddenly, all the experts are trying to be armchair quarterbacks. But I don't think they're listening to the man and woman in the street."

And on this, he may be right, at least as far as whites are concerned. A national sample of just over 1,000 adults is polled by Gallup for *Newsweek* magazine during the first two days of March, the very days when the new revelations are in the headlines. The results: 57 percent of those surveyed—up from 45 percent in mid-January—approve of Bernie's actions. And despite the news that he went back for a second shot at Cabey, two-thirds still believe he acted in self-defense. The poll shows support particularly high among men (62 percent), Republicans (63 percent), suburbanites (65 percent) and those who carry guns themselves (70 percent). When broken down by race, however, approval rate drops to 39 percent among non-whites.

But on another issue, it would seem that Bernie is the one who isn't listening. Seventy-eight percent of the women and men polled are *not* in favor of more guns on the street, saying they believe the streets would become even more dangerous than they already are if more people carried guns. Interestingly enough, 56 percent of those who carry or have carried guns share that opinion.

Another poll taken at the same time, this one co-sponsored by the New York *Daily News* and *Eyewitness News*, surveyed 505 New Yorkers and found 51 percent of all those polled in support of Bernie Goetz. When the results are tallied by race, they once again tell quite another story.

Comparing the findings of this March 1 survey with those of a similar poll taken on January 3, the analysts found that in the earlier study blacks and whites were essentially agreed: 49 percent of blacks and 52 percent of whites supported Bernie's actions. By March 1, a sharp shift was in progress, with the black approval rate dropping by 12 percent and the white rising by 5 percent: 37 percent of blacks approve compared with 57 percent of whites—very close to Gallup's national figures.

When the New Yorkers were asked in January whether they thought the subway shooter acted in self-defense, 72 percent of blacks and 77 percent of whites said yes. In March, the figures dropped to 43 percent for blacks, 60 percent for whites.

Finally, the March survey asked if Goetz should have been indicted for attempted murder. Here the difference is sharpest of all: 51 percent of blacks said yes, compared with only 19 percent of whites.

Commenting on the results, Jeff Alderman, director of the ABC polling unit responsible for the survey, notes, "The issue is definitely no longer color-blind. Blacks now disapprove of what he did; whites now approve. Blacks think he went too far and should have been indicted for attempted murder; whites don't. There were no significant differences in attitudes along racial lines in the first poll. Now there are."

February 28. Police disclose that, at the instigation of the district attorney, the search for new evidence is on in earnest.

March 1. Howard Meyer announces that Troy Canty is willing to testify without immunity if the state reopens the case against Bernie Goetz. "I want this story to come out," he says, "and I think his testimony comes under the heading of new information. Justice should be done. A grand jury should hear someone from the other side." A meeting between Canty and Assistant DA Greg Waples is set for next week, Meyer says.

As always, the experts are divided. Some lawyers wonder whether Canty's decision to testify without immunity will constitute new evidence. The prosecutor already had offered him that opportunity, so it's hard to see what would be new, they say. Even if Morgenthau should now decide to grant immunity, some legal scholars believe this still would not fit the definition of new information, since the district attorney had ample opportunity to change his mind on this while the first grand jury was still in session.

March 2. Bernie takes to the subways again, this time to take his own public opinion poll, "not from politicians but from fellow New Yorkers." Along with an editor and photographer from the *Post*, whom he has invited to join him, he enters the train at the Fourteenth Street IRT station and exits at Chambers Street, just as he did on December 22. He talks to some people, shakes hands with a dozen or so more. "Way to go, Bernie," people sing out as he passes. "I'm overwhelmed. I simply can't believe it. The support is stunning," he tells his editor companion, who publishes the story under a headline that screams: "Bernie Rides Again."

March 6. In the expectation that Troy Canty will testify, the DA asks the court for permission to open a second grand jury inquiry. Mark Baker, an associate of Barry Slotnick, petitions the judge to allow the defense to be present to argue against the reopening of the case.

March 7. Darrell Cabey awakens after seven weeks in a coma. His mother, Shirley Cabey, cries with joy. "At least he'll live." For Bernie, too, it's good news. The threat of a murder charge no longer hangs over his head.

March 7. After receiving over fifty letters threatening death and mayhem to him and his family if he testifies against Goetz, Canty considers withdrawing his promise to testify. As he begins to waver, the DA puts his request for resubmission of the case on hold.

March 9. Morgenthau meets with Troy and his mother, Eula Canty. In an effort to persuade them to reconsider, he offers to relocate them to a new home and promises police protection for the entire family. But mother and son are too frightened to agree.

March 11. Howard Meyer announces that his client will not testify. "Troy fears his family will be harmed," he explains.

When asked what this new development will do to his plan to reopen the case, the DA refuses comment.

Later that same day, James Ramseur's attorney, Ronald Kliegerman, who has been adamant on the issue of immunity, suggests that the district attorney seems to be softening his stand. If Morgenthau confers immunity, he says, his client will be happy to tell his side of the story to the grand jury.

March 12. Saying he has "significant new evidence" in his possession, the district attorney reinstates his application to reopen the case against Bernhard Goetz. Shortly thereafter, Judge Crane signs the order granting the request. The defense motion asking to be heard on the issue is denied because all matters relating to the grand jury are heard in secret.

The grand jurors, Morgenthau announces, will begin their work in a week.

30· From the Carnegie Deli to Lutèce, from the Bronx to Greenwich Village, from Brooklyn to Staten Island, the streets buzz with people talking, arguing, defending one side or the other in the case. The families of the youths who were shot are weary of it all. "Every time you think it's quietened down, it starts up again," says the father of one of the boys. "It's like you don't get a chance to forget it and live normal-like before the reporters and TV cameras are all over the place again, pushing you around and wanting to know what you think about this here new thing or that one."

At the same time, he's also glad that, from his point of view, justice will be done. "He didn't have no right to shoot those boys. They weren't doing nothing to him. Even if they done what he said, that didn't give him no right to shoot them. So, yeah, I'm glad; I think he should be punished."

For the youths themselves, a new grand jury inquiry offers the possibility of vindication. They're all too aware of the ill will so many people hold toward them. They've heard themselves described as "punks," as "hoodlums," as "thugs," as "animals" by people who never took the trouble to find out what happened between them and Bernie Goetz. They shrug it off, seeming not to care, behaving as though nothing can touch them. But they also say wonderingly, as if with all they know they still can't quite believe it, "They made up their minds before they could call our names."

As they see it, this is a society without concern for their feelings, their pain. It's as if no one has noticed they have any. So they feel abused and victimized by the press, the public, the district attorney and, of course, by Bernie Goetz and his lawyers. Not only that. They've been, in their words, "fried" for a lot less than shooting down four people. So why shouldn't he get his?

One of them, James, seems ambivalent, saying cockily one day that he hopes Goetz "fries," and another that he doesn't really wish jail on anybody, not even Bernie Goetz—a statement he is to repeat a year later after he has spent several months in jail awaiting trial on charges stemming from another case. But at the time, all three are unequivocally pleased that another grand jury inquiry is in process.

Like actors in a play, everyone else takes their accustomed places. Reporters scramble to get a lead on what the new evidence might be. Goetz supporters shout about double jeopardy and mob rule. Kelner and Slotnick accuse the DA of succumbing to political pressures and precipitating a "judicial lynching." Bernie says he's unconcerned; he knows he'll be exonerated. Morgenthau plays it cool and close to the chest. To the accusation that he has bowed to a change in public sentiment, he replies, "My mail is running nine to one for Goetz."

As the second grand jury is convened, the defense files a motion to block its work. Judge Crane refuses to halt the taking of testimony but takes the motion under advisement and gives the prosecutor one week to respond.

Meanwhile, for the first time, one of the shooting victims appears before the grand jury to tell his side of the story. James Ramseur, the first of the youths to do so, testifies under a grant of immunity from District Attorney Robert Morgenthau. The DA knows that James and Troy Canty, who will testify later, are not the most credible witnesses. Even if the grand jurors didn't know that they had been in one kind of trouble or another over the last few years, their manner, their street-wise style, would put them off. But if Morgenthau wants an indictment, he has no choice.

In an interview some weeks later, the district attorney explains his shift on immunity. "The second time around, we knew we had more factual information than before. And it was pretty clear that we didn't have any case against the kids. Without Goetz's testimony, you couldn't have a case against them.

"Then, the first time, the kids wouldn't talk to us at all. The second time, they came in and we got to hear their story and knew what they would say. To put them before a jury the first time without knowing what they'd say made no sense to us at all. And finally, the other charges that had been pending against the kids had been resolved by then, so we didn't have to worry about their getting immunity for other crimes."

James Ramseur is one of seven children—two older than he, four younger. His parents, both in their early forties, live in a long-term, stable marriage. Like so many others, they left the South, where they were born and raised, in the hope of finding a better life for themselves and their children. But it hasn't worked out that way. Indeed, it seems to them now as if nothing ever really changes, not in the South, not in the North—at least not for black folks.

It's not for lack of trying to do better that they're stuck in Claremont Village. But like so many black men, Mr. Ramseur has been able to find work only sporadically and always at low-level jobs not much different from what might have been available to him in the South if he had stayed. At the time of the shootings, he was working part-time in a pawnshop where the work is ugly and the wages are stingy. Mrs. Ramseur can't help, largely because there are too many children at home who still need her attention. So most of the time, the family is on public assistance.

James is the only one of the children who has been in trouble. But both parents insist that, until he was shot last December, they had no idea how consistent or serious the trouble might be. Sure, they knew he was caught sneaking onto the subway here and there, that he'd gotten a couple of summonses for smoking marijuana. They knew, too, that he'd been convicted of petty larceny in 1984 and spent a couple of weeks in jail. But they thought he'd learned his lesson. They didn't like any of it, but when you live in Claremont Village, you're grateful that's all.

For a few days after they heard he'd been shot, they lived in an agony of anxiety, fearful that he might die. But once the crisis passed and they knew he would live, another set of feelings came to the fore. Then they could allow themselves to feel the anger they had kept at bay. They also knew then that they had been afraid for him for a long time. But they had tried to ignore their fears, to deny the problems they could foresee but couldn't resolve.

As if to confirm their worst fears, the trouble with Bernie Goetz is not the last for James. On the evening of March 25, the police in the Bronx get an anonymous phone call telling them that James Ramseur has been kidnapped. He was seen, the caller says, being forced into a blue Cadillac by two men with guns.

Detectives from the 42nd Precinct go to his home, where his mother tells them he left the house at about four o'clock that afternoon. For the next few hours, the police canvass the neighborhood looking for clues they never find.

At 10:10 James walks into his parents' apartment. He had been driven to a playground about five miles north of Claremont Village by two men who said they were going to kill him, he tells the police, but he got away.

The police don't believe him. There are too many inconsistencies in the story he tells. So they take him down to the station house and play back for him a recording of the phone call reporting the kidnapping, suggesting to him that he had placed the call himself. Without much pressure, James admits it was all a hoax. He's charged with filing a false police report, a misdemeanor punishable by less than a year in prison and a maximum fine of $1,000.

No one can figure out why he did it, perhaps not even he. All he says is he wanted to test the police reaction.

In desperation, his parents decide to try to get him away from the Bronx, away from the people he's been around, away from the drugs he's been taking. So they send him back home, back to the farm in North Carolina, where he'll be safe, at least for a while.

But they can't keep him there very long. In a few weeks he's back on the streets heading for trouble again. Only this time, it's big trouble. On June 27, James Ramseur is arrested on charges of raping and robbing a nineteen-year-old Claremont Village woman.

According to the complaint filed by the woman who picked James out of a lineup, on May 5 he and an accomplice accosted her in the elevator of her building, forced her at gunpoint to a stairway landing near the roof of the building, raped her, and took her earrings and three rings. During the attack, they allegedly choked and beat her badly enough so that she was hospitalized for four days.

James insists he's not guilty. He and the complainant have known each other all their lives, he says. Why did she wait six weeks to pick him out of a lineup? "If James is guilty as charged, why didn't she identify him to the police when the complaint was filed?" asks his attorney.

Nevertheless, on July 9, a Bronx grand jury hands up an indictment against James Ramseur charging him with rape, robbery, sodomy, sexual abuse, assault, criminal use of a firearm and possession of stolen property. He's arraigned later that same day and bail is set at $20,000. Until the trial, he will wait in jail at Rikers Island, unable to make bail.

Almost eight months later, on March 3, 1986, James is convicted as charged. Sentencing is set for April 28. On that day, James Ramseur, now twenty years old, stands before the court and hears that he will spend the next twenty-five years in prison.

But none of these events has yet taken place when James appears before the grand jury hearing the Goetz case on a blustery March day. Immediately after his testimony, his attorney, Ronald Kliegerman, holds a news conference at his office and announces, not unexpectedly, that Ramseur's description of the events of December 22 "was in direct contradiction" to Bernie's. James acknowledges that Troy Canty approached Goetz and asked for five dollars. But with that their agreement ends. The others were still sitting down when Bernie was on his feet and started to shoot, James testified. As he told it to the grand jury, he stood up from his seat and tried to move away to avoid being shot. But there was nowhere to go. He, Barry Allen and Darrell Cabey were trapped at the end of the car when Bernie fired on them.

While the grand jurors hear testimony in one part of the building, the legal maneuvering continues in another part. The defense and prosecution are once again before Judge Crane to argue for and against the defense motion charging that the grand jury has been illegally convened. After a seventy-five-minute hearing, Judge Crane rules for the prosecution, telling Slotnick and Kelner that he "probed in detail" the new evidence before granting the request for resubmission of the case.

Angrily Slotnick argues, "This is old wine in a new bottle." To which Assistant DA Robert Pitler, appearing for the prosecution, replies, "We have a different wine and a different bottle, and this time it's champagne."

The defense moves to see the prosecution's statement of the new evidence. The judge refuses, saying, "If an indictment is handed down, you will know the nature of the evidence. If an indictment is not handed down, you will never know. I would not have permitted a new grand jury if the district attorney had been acting on a whim."

Still fighting, the defense asks that the prosecutor be instructed to present the complete videotaped statements to the grand jury rather than just portions of them. The full statements, they believe, are favorable to Goetz. And they're worried that the district attorney will make an "overzealous presentation" and not show anything that might exculpate their client. The request is denied.

Their legal moves now done and lost, Slotnick and Kelner announce that Bernie wants to testify before the grand jury. They're taking the unusual step of permitting the defendant to testify without immunity, they explain, because they fear the grand jury will be given a biased or incomplete rendering of the events of December 22.

As discussions between the defense and prosecution continue about when and how Bernie will testify, Gregory Waples gives Slotnick and Kelner until ten o'clock on Thursday, March 21, to decide if their client will in fact do so. The skeptics shrug. Again? After the on-and-off performance last time, they assume they're in for a rerun. And indeed, very soon the whole issue is caught up in controversy and delay. Bernie can't appear at the time requested by the grand jury, his attorneys say, because they need time to prepare him to testify. A delay is agreed upon. The new deadline is Monday, March 25.

Since, in this case, the person accused of the crime will waive immunity, his lawyers will be permitted to accompany him inside the grand jury room. But as the new time approaches, Barry Slotnick says he can't meet that date either because he has a conflicting court appearance. He requests a postponement until Friday, March 29, the final day of the grand jury's term. The request is refused. Once again prosecution and defense have reached a standoff.

Finally, in an attempt to end the stalemate, District Attorney Morgenthau personally appeals to the judge in the court where Slotnick is trying a nonjury case, asking him to release Slotnick from the courtroom on the appointed day so that he can accompany his client to the grand jury. The judge agrees. Morgenthau advises Slotnick that the way has been cleared, and the date is set: Bernie Goetz will present himself to the grand jury on Tuesday, March 26.

31 · While negotiations about his appearance before the grand jury drag on, Bernie spends his days talking to the press and television in what a New York *Times* reporter calls "an extraordinary news media barrage." In a most unusual move, ABC-TV's *20/20*, with Barbara Walters as anchor and Geraldo Rivera as reporter, gives over its whole hour to the case. The show not only presents Bernie Goetz live but also plays parts of the sound track from his taped New Hampshire confession.

For the first time, the public hears from Bernie's own lips something of what went on inside him during that fateful interaction in the subway. The story he tells is a familiar one by now: Troy Canty stood up, leaned over and asked him for five dollars. One of his friends joined him, and the two stood just to his left, placing themselves between him and the other passengers seated at the far end of the car. The other two moved in and stood to his right. He was surrounded. He, too, was standing by then.

At this point, the story shifts to something new, something that tells us about his internal process of evaluation and calculation. "I knew at that point I was going to have to pull the gun . . . but I wasn't going to kill them. But," he continues, "I saw the smile on his face and the shine in his eyes, that he was enjoying this. I knew then what they were going to do. Do you understand? Okay? You look, you understand now. . . . Now in combat you have to be cold-blooded. And I was. It was at that point I decided I was going to kill them all, murder them all, do anything."

Now it's Susan Braver's voice on the tape. "What did you think they were going to do?" she asks.

Bernie replies heatedly, "How can you ask a question like that? They were going to have fun with me."

Braver again: "What do you mean by that, your interpretation of that? I can't get inside your head."

Bernie, impatiently and somewhat incoherently: "Beat the shit out of me. Let me explain one thing. To do something like this, how cold-blooded it is, and you sit in your ivory tower and condemn it and say, okay, this person is a monster. You lay out your pattern of fire. Your pattern has to be from left to right in terms of detail and in terms of responsibility. You can accuse me of a lot of things, okay? Because I knew in my heart, what I—what I was. They didn't die. Well, that's what God wanted, if there's a God—that I knew in my heart I was a murderer."

Since it's a violation of the Code of Professional Responsibility for an attorney to disclose the contents of any statement made by the accused, no one involved in the case will acknowledge knowing how Rivera got the tape. But the sense of betrayal expressed by the Goetz forces after the show suggests that they may have known more about it than they're willing to admit.

"Bernie felt the whole thing was staged to sink him," reports someone close to him. And Bernie himself tells the Associated Press the next day that he had been "tricked" and "deceived" by ABC into granting the meetings with Walters and Rivera. Hearing the charge, 20/20's executive producer, Av Westin, points out that the Rivera interview was done in Joseph Kelner's office.

Kelner immediately lets it be known that he's talking to

TV people to see if he can get an unedited version of the videotape on the air to correct what he calls the "distorted picture"
the public has gotten from the edited one. Asked if this would be
in violation of the Code of Professional Responsibility, Slotnick
replies, "We are not disseminating any videotapes or any audio
tapes, but we understand that they may be disseminated by other
forces not from the defense team." At the same time, he holds a
press conference on the steps of the Criminal Courts Building,
where the grand jury is meeting. "We are publicly appealing to
the grand jury through the media to ask for all the tapes in the
case," he announces.

In another attempt to counteract the *20/20* story, the New
York *Post* headlines a front-page article titled "My Story" and,
as if to authenticate it, features an enlargement of Bernie's signa-
ture under the title. Apparently unaware of the irony of it, his
opening sentence in the story is: "This mess has been tried in
the press, on television and by the politicians.

"The public should not take as Gospel the version of *20/20*
last night," Bernie warns. And while he repeats his version of
the event, the main thrust of his story is a highly emotional and
angry attack on "the crumbling system" that's now out to get
him. "Justice appears to have been thrown out the window," he
asserts, as he keeps pointing to the criminal records of the youths,
to the screwdrivers in their pockets. "I walk into a subway train,
and I am victimized. Now, look at it. I am being sued for
millions of dollars by the likes of Mr. Canty and Mr. Cabey,
men who are not unfamiliar with police records or theft. I mean,
here is the thing. I make money out of being an engineer. How
does Mr. Canty make his money?"

It's true that Troy Canty long ago learned the ways of the
petty crimes that would get him enough money to be a "man"
on the street, enough also to buy the drugs that would dull his
brain and dim his conscience. But his offenses have all been for
crimes against property, none for violent crimes or crimes against
persons. Certainly such young men often enough move from

relatively minor crimes to major ones without giving warning. But do we have a right to punish them in advance, just in case? Perhaps more crucial, when Bernie Goetz pulled his gun and fired five bullets into the bodies of four young men, he knew nothing of their criminal records, had never seen the screwdrivers in their pockets.

Was Troy high on drugs when he approached Bernie? Probably. Was he a danger to him? Bernie says yes; Troy says no. Both are answers we'd expect. Troy says, "He sat down opposite me and kept staring at us, me especially." Was this his paranoia born of too much cocaine? Or was his perception an accurate one? Bernie says he was just sitting there minding his own business.

Was it his drug-induced euphoria that emboldened Troy to try to get five dollars from Bernie, whether by request or demand, depending upon who tells the story? Probably. Would he have hurt him if Bernie had told him to buzz off? Troy says no; Bernie says yes. Again no surprise.

But there's something peculiarly convincing about Troy, and something pathetic, even while also frightening. He knows that many people think of him as someone not fully human, that Bernie Goetz has become a hero for having shot him. He knows, too, that at least some of those people are sorry he recovered from his wounds. And like the man who fired the gun, he has a complicated set of feelings about it all.

Somewhere inside he's hurt at being viewed as an animal. But he'll never let "those motherfuckers" know it. So in a quite human defensive maneuver, he covers the hurt with anger and swaggers about boastfully as he makes his way around the social rules and conventions that bind the rest of us.

Yet he's not without fear also. In his more rational moments, when he's not in a drug-induced haze which allows him to believe in his own invulnerability, he's plenty scared—scared of living and scared of dying. But in the world he lives in, fear is a dangerous emotion, a setup for disaster, for being victimized on those perilous streets he must travel every day. So again, nobody knows. Too often, he doesn't know himself, won't allow such feelings into consciousness. At least not until they force their way in at the sight of a gun in a man's hand.

Would he have backed off even before he saw Bernie's gun? He insists the answer is yes. He's done plenty of dumb things in his life, he agrees. But this happened in the middle of the afternoon, in broad daylight. And there were people all around. He's not that crazy.

It's easy to believe that Bernie didn't feel he could rid himself of Troy that easily. But surely he must have known that the show of the gun would have been enough to send chills of fear through his antagonist. "Don't shoot, man; it's cool," Troy tried to say when he saw the gun. But the bullets came too fast; the words never got past his lips.

But perhaps by then Bernie was too frightened to care about anything but protecting himself. In that case, wouldn't shooting just one of the youths have done the trick? Self-defense, Bernie says. Yet he shot two people in the back, one with a second shot when he was already down and cowering in his seat. And if the gun he carried was just a defensive weapon, why was it loaded with hollow-point bullets—ammunition designed to inflict maximum damage?

Or was it vengeance he sought? "If I was thinking a little bit more clearly," he told Detective Domian when asked about having delivered the second shot to Darrell Cabey, "I would have put the barrel against his forehead and fired."

"I walked over to the guy who had talked to me," he said, speaking of Troy Canty as he lay on the floor. "I wanted to look at his eyes. I don't even want to say what may have been in my mind. I looked at his eyes, though, and there was such fear—you know, the look had changed. . . . I just said to him in a mean voice, 'This better be a lesson to you.'"

Was he speaking only to Troy? Or were both words and deeds also an angry acting out of a quiet rage that had been tormenting him since childhood? "I saw the smile on his face and the shine in his eyes that he was enjoying this," he told Susan Braver during questioning at police headquarters in Concord. Like the kids in the schoolyard who smiled and shone when they sent him home in tears of helpless rage?

"They were going to have fun with me," he said a moment later. Not hit me or hurt me, not maim me or kill me. "They were going to have *fun* with me." Like the kids who had "fun" with him when they teased and humiliated him beyond endurance? Like the boys in Rhinebeck had "fun" when they accused his father and watched the family flee in disgrace?

32. As the tumult continues to escalate outside the grand jury room, inside, the jurors go quietly about their work. They hear the testimony of Troy Canty, who essentially affirms the story Ramseur told earlier, adding only that from the minute Goetz boarded the train, he kept staring at them as if looking for a fight.

On the same day, Victor Flores, a burly forty-seven-year-old father of six who lives in the Bronx and has worked as a porter for the Transit Authority for twenty years, also appears before the grand jury. In an interview immediately after giving his testimony, Flores, a passenger on the train when the shooting broke out, says in a voice trembling with emotion, "After it happened, even when I was sleeping, I would wake up thinking about it. A lot of nights I couldn't sleep just thinking about what happened."

His first thought on hearing the shots, Flores recalls, was that Goetz was a police officer. When he realized he wasn't, he was terrified, wondering, "Am I next? Is he going to shoot everyone?" His stomach was so tightly knotted with fear and the pain so excruciating, he says, that "I thought for a minute maybe I was hit too.

"I told the grand jury I don't think there was any reason for that shooting." Sure, the teenagers were noisy, Flores acknowledges, but he never saw them menace anyone. "I told them that I didn't feel threatened by anyone."

In describing the actual shooting itself, he said that Goetz supported himself against the upright pole near the end of the car and fired at three of the youths as they ran toward its center. "I saw the three kids in front of me go down—boom, boom, boom. . . . The kids were real close to Goetz. When Goetz was shooting he looked professional. He wasn't sloppy. He knew what he was doing."

When the shooting stopped, Flores told the grand jurors, one of the youths was slumped on a seat across from the conductor's booth at the end of the car. Another was on the seat opposite, and the third and fourth were lying next to each other on the floor. He watched Bernie kneel down and examine one of them, he said, but he didn't see him go back for another shot. As Bernie was moving away from the scene, Flores heard one of the boys on the floor repeating, "He did it for nothin'; we weren't doing nothin'."

The story Flores tells is powerful. But it's inconsistent with the version Ramseur and Canty have given. According to the youths, only Canty was standing when Goetz pulled his gun. Ramseur testified that he stood up when the shooting started and tried to move away, but he and the others couldn't escape because Goetz had them trapped at the end of the car. Flores, however, says that three of the boys were shot as they tried to run toward the center of the car.

Internally, too, Flores's story is contradictory. When the shooting stopped, he testified, two of the boys were slumped on the benches opposite each other at the far end of the car, two others were on the floor. If three of them were shot when they were fleeing toward the center of the car, how could two have been found seated in the corner?

Such contradictions are to be expected, of course. The boys have a stake in the story and will tell it to their advantage. And eyewitness testimony is notoriously variable and often unreliable, especially in a situation as anxiety-provoking as this one surely was for the innocent people caught in it. But these inconsistencies become particularly troubling in this case because of the passions and controversy it has stirred.

The day Bernie Goetz is scheduled to testify before the grand jury finally arrives. Taking every possible precaution, the district attorney orders the entire complex housing his office and the Criminal Courts Building sealed off. Press and public will be barred for the day.

At 8:30 a.m. on Tuesday, March 26, Bernie arrives at the DA's office with Barry Slotnick. Two hours later, they emerge angrily. "The district attorney refused our testimony," Slotnick announces to the crush of reporters and photographers awaiting the news.

The defense, it seems, asked that the inquiry be limited only to the events of December 22, the day of the shootings, and December 30, the day Goetz turned the guns over to his neighbor for safekeeping. The prosecution refused. Slotnick charges the district attorney with trying to stack the deck against his client.

In response, Morgenthau issues a written statement in which he gives a point-by-point accounting of the events from March 13, when the DA's office advised Goetz's attorneys that a new grand jury investigation was beginning. Morgenthau explains that he sent Slotnick the standard waiver-of-immunity form for Bernie to sign on March 21, and that it wasn't until Monday, March 25, that any question about it was raised. Since a limited waiver of immunity would, in the DA's words, "restrict the grand jury's access to information," Morgenthau advised Slotnick at once that he "could not accede to this demand," the statement concludes. Beyond this, Morgenthau will not elaborate.

Slotnick, however, has plenty to say, insisting that the district attorney's refusal to agree to a limited waiver of immunity is incomprehensible. But legal experts all say that it couldn't have come as a surprise to Barry Slotnick. Every criminal lawyer knows, they explain, that prosecutors generally don't permit the subjects of grand jury investigations to set the conditions for their testimony.

At the height of the uproar, Slotnick releases a letter written by Bernie and addressed to the foreman of the grand jury. "I beg of you," the letter reads, "to allow me to come into the grand jury room so that you will hear the whole truth about the horrors that I faced at the hands of other of your witnesses who have received the benefit of full immunity."

But this, too, must have been written more for the media than for the grand jury. It was written on Monday, the day *before* his scheduled appearance and *after* the DA had refused the conditions the defense sought to impose. Moreover, Slotnick would surely have known such a letter would never reach its destination, since it is the district attorney, not the grand jurors, who decides the conditions under which a witness will appear. Indeed, it would have been unheard of for Gregory Waples, to whom the letter was delivered, to pass it on.

In a column in the *Post* the next day, Beth Fallon writes: "What we had at 100 Centre St. yesterday in the Bernhard Goetz case was your basic charade. The Goetz defense team didn't really want their man to testify before the grand jury. And he didn't. And if you want my hunch, District Attorney Robert Morgenthau didn't really want Goetz to testify, either. And he didn't. So probably everybody's happy, and the Great Waiver Controversy is a nice place for everybody to put the blame."

In an interview some weeks later Morgenthau says, "We never expected him to testify. That was just a matter of public relations by the defense lawyers to try to make us look bad and as if we were being tough on the hero." And when asked whether he ever meant to let Bernie testify, Slotnick responds with an enigmatic smile and a question: "What do you think?"

33· On March 27, the grand jury throws the book at Bernhard Goetz. He is indicted on four counts of attempted murder in the second degree, four counts of assault in the first degree, one count of criminal possession of a weapon in the second degree and one count of reckless endangerment in the first degree. A telephone repairman snarls, "The goddamn animals won again. Instead of America the beautiful, we've got America the crazy. It's a damn shame." William Kunstler, one of Cabey's lawyers, sighs with relief: "The indictment is the first step back on the road to sanity in this case."

Within twenty-four hours, a pale, downcast and weary Bernie surrenders to the police. For the third time in three months, he's booked and fingerprinted at police headquarters; for the third time, he's led handcuffed through a maze of reporters and cameramen into the Criminal Courts Building at 100 Centre Street for arraignment. In court, handcuffs removed, he stands quietly through the fifty-minute hearing, hands folded before him, eyes glued to the floor.

After entering a not guilty plea on behalf of his client, Barry Slotnick advises the court that he will move to dismiss the indictment on the ground that the second grand jury was improperly convened. Since New York law requires a judge to hear a motion to dismiss, Justice Crane gives the defense forty-five days, until May 16, to file the papers. That accomplished, Slotnick also asks Justice Crane to remove himself from the case. He acted improperly in signing the order initiating the second grand jury, the defense attorney contends. The judge denies the request, saying huffily, "If I should recuse myself because of any appearance of impropriety, I will act on my own motion."

Now the problem of fixing bail is taken up. The defense, of course, urges that bail remain at $5,000. "He has nowhere to go, Judge; he has nowhere to flee," pleads Slotnick. "Unfortunately, he has the best-known face in the country." The prosecutor, agreeing that Goetz is not likely to flee, nevertheless asks for $20,000 cash bail. "Your honor is aware of the new evidence," Waples reminds the court, "and that in fact there is a substantial basis for the new charges." This time Justice Crane finds for the defense. Bail remains fixed at $5,000.

Finally the story of the subway vigilante is no longer in the news. For the first time in over three months, there's not a daily story in the press. The noise around this case has been long and loud. For most people, the quiet is a relief. Let a jury of his peers decide.

34. For Bernie, the quiet that descends after the second grand jury hands up its indictments is not so simple. For the private side of the split inside him, it surely must bring some relief from the never-ending press of publicity, from knowing that, unless he proceeds with the utmost caution, his every word and deed will be recorded and reported. But he's had plenty of that kind of privacy in the past, enough to last a couple of lifetimes. And the part of him that has reveled in being noticed, in being heard, in becoming a public figure of substance and note, seems to have trouble tolerating the silence again.

So two weeks after his last arraignment, he announces plans to place ads in major newspapers around the country to appeal for contributions to his Defense Fund. The expenses in the case continue to mount, he says, and he needs help from a public that has shown its support.

But the public is fickle. The announcement is met with cynicism, as people recall that the man who once refused all help now plans to solicit money from a grateful public. The ads never appear, and this is the last anyone hears about the plan.

Still the transformation of Bernie Goetz continues. As the weeks pass, the public man wins out over the private one. More and more, he seems to turn outward. One day neighbors find him sitting cross-legged on the floor in the hallway in front of his apartment as he is being interviewed by a reporter. If he notices his neighbors' annoyance as they walk by shaking their heads and muttering their disapproval, he gives no sign. "He didn't pay any attention at all to the fact that people are fed up with him and his bizarre behavior," says one of those who passed the scene.

Carole Agus, the *Newsday* reporter who sits with him, notices. Their irritated glances make her even more uncomfortable than her awkward position on the floor. At the same time, like so many others who have tried to talk to Bernie about the shootings—indeed about anything but electronics—she has become impatient with his talk. His habit of speaking in abstractions, his penchant for broad generalizations, for statements whose meanings are obscure, make the conversation seem like one big riddle. His intelligence is undoubted, she writes later. But it's "intelligence like a filmstrip: visible and audible, but not interactive. He is bursting with strong opinions lacking insight, devoid of introspection. Asking Goetz to explain himself is like asking a computer why it works."

People who have been his neighbors for years comment in astonishment about the difference in the person they see now and the one they used to know. "He was very unlike the person you now see on TV," says one woman. "It just appears that he started to like the notoriety, and although he disclaims that, it seems to be the case. He was around before, but he wasn't ever involved with other people like he is now. And you never saw as much of him as you do now. It's not just a little bit more, either; it's like ten times more.

"Last week I saw him in the lobby entertaining two policemen, and I was outraged. There are plenty of problems on Fourteenth Street that need police attention, and they didn't have to be in the lobby being entertained by Bernie." With a sigh: "But he's a celebrity now, and they love it. And as long as there's someone to listen, Bernie's there these days talking and laughing and kidding around like you never saw before. It's like he's holding court."

Another neighbor who has observed Bernie closely for several years comments: "He hardly ever had anyone in his apartment before the incident, at least not friends. He was the most private person I ever saw; I don't know if he ever had a friend before this. Mostly the people who came were customers. You'd know that because they'd come carrying the equipment they wanted him to fix. Now there seem to be a lot of people coming and going—people who appear to be supporters. And I get the impression that he loves it.

"He's very much more present and social now. Before, he was absolutely antisocial. If you said good morning to him, maybe he'd respond and maybe he wouldn't. If you said, 'How are you today?' he'd laugh or giggle in that funny way he has, as if you'd asked him a crazy question. Or sometimes he'd seem to be responding to you, but he wasn't answering the question you asked. He'd say something totally off, as if he had a whole other conversation going on in his head.

"Now if you meet him in the hall or the elevator, he's quite friendly and very talkative, very animated. I don't mean he makes sense a lot of the time; he doesn't. But he's obviously more comfortable in social settings. It's hard to believe it's the same person. He must have been playing out in his own mind the scripts for how to be a social person all these years, because he couldn't have just emerged this way. It's like two different people."

But it's not two different people. It's different sides of the same person, made possible by the fact that, in all of us, the entity we call "a self" is a complex integration of various facets of our personality. Each new set of experiences taps some part of the self—sometimes a part that is already relatively well developed, sometimes one that has been subordinated to the more dominant parts of our personality, sometimes one that is unseen and unknown until it is called up in response to the experience under way.

As events have moved Bernie out of his dark private world and into the spotlight, the social part of his self, which before was so inchoate, begins to grow and develop. Oftentimes, when such dramatic changes occur in a person, it seems as if this now is the functioning whole, as if the other was just a sham, a false self developed to hide the real one. But it isn't so. Not for Bernie, not for any of us. Rather, the person we knew is still alive and well. But for the moment at least, there's a new balance in the way the various parts of self find expression. Whether this new equilibrium becomes integrated into a stable presentation of self, only time and the experiences to come will tell.

Watching Bernie one day as he comes striding out of his lawyer's private office and through the reception room, it's easy to see what people mean about the changes in him. He seems to have grown straighter and taller now than he used to be. He walks more erectly, his head up, a jaunty spring to his step.

He stops for a moment before a secretary's desk and, somewhat awkwardly but with a warm smile, makes some small talk. She responds in kind. But the repartee is quickly exhausted, and he stands uncertainly, not knowing how to take his leave. A few awkward seconds pass, and he moves on.

He smiles at the visitor waiting in the reception area as he passes through, a smile that says he knows he's been recognized, that he doesn't mind, indeed, rather likes it. Then without breaking stride, he opens the heavy oak door that leads to the public hallway and leaves.

Seconds later, the outer door swings open again and he re-enters, saying gaily to anyone who will listen, "I forgot to tell

Barry something." He moves easily through the public area and into the private regions beyond. No need for announcements; he knows he'll be welcomed.

The sounds of male laughter filter through, a voice is raised in command: "Don't forget to see that Bernie gets a copy of that file!" A murmur of assent follows. Soon after, Bernie emerges once again. A small comment to the same secretary, another smile to the waiting visitor, and he leaves once more.

But like a child who can't quite pull himself away from the bosom of the family, he's still not gone. Seconds later, he comes through the outside door yet again, hurries through the front offices, this time looking somewhat abashed, and disappears.

Is he looking uncomfortable now because he understands that this is not just his forgetfulness, that he can't leave because he doesn't want to go? Does he know that it's hard for him to leave the warmth and comradeship he finds here for the quiet emptiness of his daily life at home?

Again there's the sound of male voices bantering and the words: "Take one! Sure, go ahead, as many as you want." Another minute or two pass before Bernie reappears, this time with a blissful smile on his face. In each hand, he carries a cookie. The one in his left hand is just coming away from his mouth as he takes a bite. The other sits cupped in his right palm, which he carries before him as a child holds a treasure—the arm pressed tightly to his body, the hand slightly forward, fingers curled to protect the cherished object.

He walks forward more slowly this time; the cargo is precious. But now he'll be able to leave. Like the small child who drags a blanket around for comfort, he has something to take with him, something to warm him on the journey home, to remind him that he's loved—what psychologists call a transitional object.

It's not just a child who walks by, however. Rather it's half child/half man. The child's face is lit with delight, it's true. He has been fed—in both the real and the metaphoric sense. But the adult is watching also. And this part of Bernie seems to stand momentarily apart from the scene and reflect upon it. So he looks around as he passes through, shrugs self-consciously as if to say, "I know, I know," and finally departs for good.

35. For over thirteen months, 411 long days, Darrell Cabey's home will be an eight-by-twelve-foot hospital room. It's a depressing room, cluttered with hospital paraphernalia, impersonal and cold, even after his long residence in it.

During most of his stay, he has been bedridden. But in the few months before his release on February 6, 1986, he's able to move around in a wheelchair. Sometimes he goes down to the patients' recreation room and hangs out with others there. But mostly he watches television from morning until night because there's not much else he can do. With the brain damage he has suffered, he can't read even the automotive magazines he used to like so much.

He handles his wheelchair relatively easily now, but he has to be careful. The paralysis, it turns out, doesn't start at the waist but above it. So the upper half of his body is unstable, in danger of toppling unless it's protected. The rehabilitation specialists who have worked so hard with him have ordered a special chair, one that's designed to hold him safely in place. But until it arrives, when he's in motion one arm lies across his body, the hand gripping the arm of the chair—like a strap that secures him firmly in the seat.

. . .

On November 25, *Daily News* columnist Jimmy Breslin visits Darrell in the hospital, the first reporter to be permitted to see him since he was wounded eleven months ago. After he leaves, Breslin writes a column in which he quotes Darrell as saying about his companions, "They were goin' to rob him. They thought he looked like easy bait." But he, Darrell, left the subway car because he didn't want to be involved, according to the story he told Breslin. "Where were you when [the shooting] happened?" Breslin asked. "I came back to the car. I sat down a couple of seats away. I wasn't with them."

The news is sensational. "I told you so," Goetz's partisans exult. "It's just like Bernie has been saying all along." His lawyers smile happily. They soon won't have to worry about Bernie's defense if these kids keep talking. Others, those whose sympathies are on the other side, say glumly, "It would have been hard enough to find a jury to convict him before. Now he'll walk for sure."

In the same column Breslin reports having asked Darrell if he could remember "going through the turnstile." "Turnstile on 14th Street," Darrell answered. When he was reminded that he got on the train in the Bronx, he said, "We were traveling. I think so." He "seemed confused," Breslin writes, and "questioning had to be sparse" because he "was having some trouble in speaking [and] became uneasy when I attempted to ask him about something a second time, or when I asked him something too rapidly."

But neither the headlines nor the news stories that follow the publication of this column comment on the obvious confusion in Darrell's responses or, for that matter, ask questions of any kind. Yet anyone who knows the subway line on which the incident took place knows also that it takes just over three minutes for the train to get from Fourteenth Street to its next stop at Chambers Street. The action had to take place in less time than that.

Does it make sense that, in three minutes, Bernie could have sat down, the boys looked him over, made a decision to rob him, somehow communicated the plan to each other and initiated the action; that Darrell then could have left the car, walked to the next one, thought it over and decided to come back, walked back to the first car and sat down again in time for Bernie to shoot him; that Bernie would still have time to check out each one of the youths where he fell, shoot Darrell a second time, sit down for a moment or two, get up and walk through the car to make sure none of the other passengers was hurt and leave the train? Responding to the question, Breslin says, "Come on! He was trying to separate himself from them so they could win a lawsuit and get some dough from Goetz. Listen, I know Goetz lured them into it. But this story the kid's telling now is a lot of crap."

If Darrell's aim is simply to strengthen his lawsuit, why would he say the others were out to rob Goetz at all? Why not just keep quiet about it? "How the hell do I know? I do what I do, and I've been doing it for thirty-four years. I got it in writing. He said it; that's all there is to it."

The day after the Breslin story appears, the prosecution takes another blow. A police officer named Peter Smith, one of the first on the scene after the shootings, comes forward to say that, while still in the subway car, Troy Canty told him, "We were going to rob him, but he shot us first." His sudden appearance delights the defense and puzzles both the prosecution and at least some members of the police department. Where was he until now? they ask. If his story is true, why is there no entry to this effect in his memo book, as standard police procedure requires?

In separate interviews, first with two detectives, then with the prosecutor, Officer Smith is asked if he had ever given this information to his supervisor or to any investigator on the case. He says, unequivocally, he had not. But a few days later, when talking again with Assistant DA Gregory Waples—this time with an attorney from the policemen's union present—Smith changes his story. Now he says that, on the day of the shootings, he told Detective Michael Clark about Canty's remark—a statement Clark emphatically denies.

Police Commissioner Benjamin Ward expresses doubt about the truth of Smith's statements and asks for a departmental investigation. And although the prosecution is highly skeptical about his story, they worry that, just because Smith is a police officer, he could be a damaging witness when the case comes to trial. It becomes more essential than ever, therefore, for them to establish just what Darrell Cabey remembers and whether he can be a credible witness.

On Friday, December 20, two days short of the first anniversary of the shootings, Gregory Waples talks to Darrell Cabey. According to his mother, who was present during the interview, Darrell assured Waples that he remembered what happened. But when pressed for details, he became confused and answered either vaguely or incorrectly. In response to a question that asked who else was on the train besides Goetz, Darrell said "Nobody." When asked if he remembered where he, his companions and Goetz were sitting, he said, "Yes." But when Waples put before him a diagram of the subway car and asked him to show where everyone was, Darrell moved his hand over the page uncertainly and, after a moment or two, put all the actors in the drama, including himself, in the wrong place.

There's no fruitful way to question such discrepancies, to remind Darrell that there were over twenty other passengers in that subway car, to show him where he was actually found after he had been shot. For when he's confronted with such evidence of his disability, he becomes agitated and confused. His language, primitive at best, deserts him almost entirely; his words become so garbled that he can be almost impossible to understand.

In this conversation with Waples, his mind quickly became so clouded that his mother, who unquestionably understands him better than anyone else, says, "Even I got confused and didn't know what he was talking about."

December 22—one year since the shootings. It's hard to stay in the hospital room with Darrell for very long—hard to feel the confines of its walls, to imagine what it would be like to live here for so long. It's hard to see the tubes poking out from beneath the legs of his pants, to wonder what it would be like to know that this is for life. It's hard to hear his labored speech, to watch the effort he makes to appear normal, to see the frustration that follows when he hasn't made himself understood.

It took months of painful effort for him to learn to say even the simplest words again. He can do better than that now, but not unless he's perfectly calm. And a visitor, any visitor except those most familiar to him, makes him tense and anxious. That tension often translates itself into a sullen withdrawal that makes this once good-looking kid anything but attractive.

On this day, in the kind of chitchat that goes on in hospital rooms, he's asked if he's tired of life in the hospital and eager to get home. His mother, who has become accustomed to covering for him, protecting him, interpreting for him, tries to smooth the way by answering before he has a chance to. "Oh," she says smilingly, "Darrell thinks this *is* home."

But Darrell responds as if he's been hit, the angry frustration that lies simmering inside him now out of his control. One hand pushing at the air, he shouts, "No, do' say 'at; do' say it." A few moments of surprised silence during which Mrs. Cabey looks resigned and the visitor uncomfortable, then another question: Does he know where his real home is? But now he sits in his wheelchair looking down at the floor, his face set in an unresponsive mask. There's no way to know what he knows. For the moment, he's nursing his anger and pain and isn't talking at all.

He seems to come back into the interaction after a while. "Do you like football, Darrell?" A shrug. What does it mean? Another try: "Too bad the Jets lost, isn't it?" Now he shakes his head as if to clear it, and finally offers an unintelligible response. "Sorry, I couldn't hear you, Darrell. What'd you say?" As if with great effort, he mobilizes himself and, speaking slowly and painfully, says, "I do' li' foo'ba'."

His doctors say he has the mental capacity of an eight-year-old. But that tells only part of the story. For he hasn't simply reverted to being eight. Rather he now has an eight-year-old mind living in a body with a nineteen-year history—the history of a person who, until one year ago, functioned perfectly normally.

He's less like a retarded child, therefore, than an old person who has given way to senility. And, as with a senile one, memories return, fragments from incidents that had meaning at some earlier time. One here, one there, like a scene from a dream—each one part of some larger context that's no longer available to him, each one separated from the other in real life by time and space. But for him, there is no longer any "real life" in the past; there is only the life he can construct in his mind with all its present limitations.

And construct it he must. It's part of his human need to make sense of his environment, to give meaning to his life. So out of the bits and pieces of memory that come to him, he creates a story that's more or less coherent and, for him, it becomes the reality. A memory of his father when he was five becomes fused with a memory of a family outing when he was twelve. They are no longer two events, but one.

When he says, "I remember," therefore, no one can know what he actually recalls. Sometimes it may be these real memories around which he has written his own narrative. At other times it will be a construction from stories told to him about his past. We've all done it. We retell an incident from childhood and think, "I don't really know if I remember it or if it just seems like my memory because I've heard the story so often." But for Darrell, it's not just a single incident that's in question, it's most of his life.

He's heard the story of the shootings, of course. His mother has told him as much as she knows about what happened that day on the subway train. He's listened to any number of reports on TV and radio. What part of what he knows is recall and what has been manufactured from what he's heard? We'll probably never know.

What we do know is that his damaged brain has a limited capacity to process information. In his mother's words: "He gets mixed up when he hears things sometimes, especially when it's about him or Goetz. I'm always explaining something to him, but no matter how much I try, he still doesn't really understand. One day they were saying on the news that they dropped some old robbery charges against him, and he thought he heard them say he hurt somebody or their family or something. I never could understand exactly what he thought he heard. He was all upset, though, and kept asking me, 'Mama, what'd they say I did; who'd I hurt?' I kept trying to tell him they didn't say anything like that because he never did hurt no one. But he was so confused and upset, I couldn't make him understand."

We know, also, that as part of the human imperative to make sense of the world, he'll continue to try to understand what happened to his life by fashioning a script with which he can live. It's comparable to what happens with a young child who, for example, wants to know how the baby got into mommy's stomach. Mother replies by saying that daddy planted a seed, a response that seems to satisfy the little one. Weeks later, mother is astonished to hear the complicated—and inaccurate—story the child has constructed out of this lone bit of information.

So it is with Darrell. He tailors some idiosyncratic combination of fact and fantasy into a story he can comprehend. But it's also different for him than it is for a child. The child has the capacity to learn as it grows, to modify the story so that it becomes progressively closer to reality. For Darrell, that possibility is gone. His damaged brain will never grow beyond the eight-year-old capability that is now his.

"I think about how crazy this whole thing is all the time," sighs Shirley Cabey. "Darrell's name will be in the history books. Imagine getting into the history books this way!"

36· It's now the end of January 1986, thirteen months since the shootings, and no trial date has yet been set. Since the second grand jury issued its indictments, the defense has kept the case moving through the courts with a series of motions for dismissal. When the last of these appeals was rejected by the Court of Appeals, New York's highest court, Barry Slotnick took the case back to the State Supreme Court with a new set of motions. This time he argued, among other things, that the DA "prejudiced the integrity of the grand jury" when he instructed the jurors to consider how a reasonable person in Goetz's position would have been expected to react rather than what Bernie alone might have been thinking and feeling in his encounter with the four youths.

On January 16, Justice Stephen Crane finds for the defense and dismisses two of the four charges against Bernie, those for assault and attempted murder. The charges for illegal weapons possession and reckless endangerment—that is, the possibility that innocent bystanders could have been wounded—are left standing. The ruling is based on the judge's assessment that there was prejudicial error in the prosecutor's instructions on the law of self-defense, and that the testimony of Troy Canty and James Ramseur was perjured. His opinion that the youths had lied to the grand jury rests on Officer Peter Smith's recent statement that Troy told him they were planning to rob Goetz, and on Jimmy Breslin's report of his interview with Darrell Cabey.

To support his decision that the district attorney had erred in instructing the grand jurors, Justice Crane cited, among others, a United States Supreme Court decision written by Oliver Wendell Holmes. "If a man reasonably believes that he is in immediate danger of death or grievous bodily harm from his assailant he may stand his ground, and if he kills him he has not exceeded the bounds of lawful self-defense. . . . Detached reflection cannot be demanded in the presence of an uplifted knife," wrote Justice Holmes. But not even Goetz himself claims to have been threatened by any weapon at all, let alone by one so deadly as "an uplifted knife."

The implications of Crane's ruling are of profound importance, not just for the criminal justice system but for the larger society as well. If this interpretation of the New York law on self-defense is left to stand, any person could justify murder if he claimed to believe he was about to be attacked and couldn't get away. No matter that the law requires that a *reasonable* belief must be established. The crucial issue would be whether, in the murderer's own subjective judgment, he honestly believed he was at risk. Whether that belief was right or wrong, whether it stemmed from paranoia or prejudice, would be irrelevant. As District Attorney Robert Morgenthau says, "A subjective standard justifies any use of deadly force, even under circumstances which almost everyone in the community would think inappropriate."

Nevertheless, if Bernhard Goetz is to stand trial for assault and attempted murder, the DA will have to win an appeal from this ruling or put the case before a third grand jury. By now, even the most diehard Goetz opponent must begin to wonder if the latter wouldn't constitute cruel and unusual punishment. Morgenthau announces that he will appeal.

Three months later, the Appellate Division renders its opinion.

In a 3-to-2 decision, the lower court's dismissal of the assault and attempted murder charges is upheld. But the court stresses that the issue at bar was not Goetz's guilt or innocence. "The sole issue is the propriety of the instructions by the assistant district attorney to the grand jury," the majority asserts.

Still, the legal maneuverings are not at an end. Once again, the DA will appeal, this time to New York's court of last resort, the Court of Appeals.

On July 8, the High Court delivers its unanimous opinion that the Lower Court's interpretation of the law of self-defense is in error. In reinstating all the charges against Goetz, Chief Judge Sol Wachtler writes: "To completely exonerate such an individual would allow citizens to set their own standards for the permissible use of force. It would also allow a legally competent defendant [who is] suffering from delusions to kill or perform acts of violence with impunity, contrary to fundamental principles of justice and criminal law."

Finally, almost nineteen months after the New York subway shootings burst into public consciousness, the decision is in: Bernhard Hugo Goetz will stand trial for assault, attempted murder, reckless endangerment and illegal weapons possession.

37. The social issues this case has raised are larger than the outcome of the appeals and the counter-appeals, larger even than the verdict of a trial jury. Certainly the problem of street crime that so plagues us today is in itself a compelling one, and justly so. Without doubt the experience of recent years, the fear of walking the streets and riding the subways, has played a part in the intensity of the public response, in the ambivalence that even anti-Goetz people feel about him and his behavior. Indeed, in important ways, the case has touched the contradictory parts in us, just as it has in Goetz himself—the "monster" part, to use his own word for his actions, and the decent, gentle one; the part that would like to be able to "stand up and be counted" as he did, and the one that looks with dismay, if not horror, at his behavior. In allowing his "monster" part to act, Bernie Goetz did for us what we could not, would not, do for ourselves. This is why so many of us could feel such sympathy with him even when we didn't wholly approve what he had done.

But the enormous rage this case has let loose requires an explanation beyond our fears of our own victimization and our anxiety about our helplessness. It is related also to a set of contradictions that inhere in our society and in our lives—in a society that once seemed so open and that has suddenly, inexplicably, closed down; in a nation where the median family income for whites is $21,902, yet where most people are so heavily in debt that even a temporary disruption in their paycheck would be devastating; in the peculiar paradox of an affluent middle class that *feels* poor because it cannot afford decent housing, especially in cities like New York; in a history of racism for which we are now being called upon to pay the price.

Both economically and socially, we feel ourselves at risk. The economic retrenchment of recent years threatens the affluence to which so many Americans have become accustomed, leaving us frightened and insecure, fearful of poverty, even as we live in the midst of plenty. The breakdown of social order, the emerging understanding that there will never be enough police to enforce the law in a society where some significant number of people refuse to respect it, threatens the very basis of our daily lives and leaves us feeling hopelessly out of control.

But we cannot tolerate the knowledge of our own powerlessness, so we defend against it with our rage. A rage that seeks revenge for every pain experienced, for every promise not met, for every paint-smeared train or bus, for every moment of fear. A rage that has no easy target, therefore finds expression in a script that pits the dark barbarians against the brave, blond knight.

But the case of Bernhard Goetz and the youths he shot is no simple matter of good versus evil, of one law-abiding white man against four killer blacks. Rather this is the version that fits the imagery about blacks our history has bequeathed to us—images that lie deep inside the American psyche, easily tapped by an event such as this one. So easily, in fact, that millions of good citizens unquestioningly accepted the notion that Bernie Goetz *reasonably* believed he was in danger of "grievous bodily harm" from the two youths he shot in the back—one who ran at the sight of the gun, the other who sat cringing in his seat as Bernie put a point-blank second shot into his body. So easily that even a judge in New York's State Supreme Court saw a threat from "an uplifted knife" where there was none.

Yet it's also true that we have reason to fear. For the first time in our history, it is the white pulse that quickens in fear at the sound of footsteps on a darkened street; it is white feet that hurry across to the other side at the sight of blacks ahead. Suddenly, we have no way to protect ourselves; we are no longer in control. It makes no difference whether we're "good guys" or "bad guys"; we're all equally vulnerable. It's the anonymous "honky" who's now under attack, just as throughout our history it has been the nameless "nigger."

This is what stirs our fears so deeply, this experience of a fundamentally new sense of vulnerability. And the knowledge, however much denied, that we get back what we have given. For the hatred, the lack of human pity, we see in the eyes of the young blacks who lash out so furiously is but a reflection of the view we have mirrored to them for so long.

There are no excuses for these violent youths, not in the white world, not in the black one. They have made all of our lives, especially those of their black neighbors, a nightmare of anxiety and fear. We no longer feel safe in our homes, on our streets, in our subways and buses. Indeed, except for our homes, the rest are no longer ours. It's just this that makes us so angry, that seems such an outrage. *They* have taken over *our* public places while we hide in fear. The only safety left to us are locked doors and barred windows. And often enough, these don't protect us either. Society's historic victims have become its victimizers.

Observing anew the streets of Harlem about which he wrote twenty years ago, Claude Brown, author of *Manchild in the Promised Land*, now tells us what we have already guessed and feared about "Manchild 1984." He's colder, harder, meaner, more persistently violent than any we have ever known before. He'll take what he wants when he wants it and doesn't really care if he gives up his life to get it. He'd seem pathetic if he weren't so altogether terrifying.

Nothing matters—not living, not dying. But if he must live, he'll do it on his terms, not ours. Sometimes he'll rob and steal because he wants the money to buy some dope or maybe the right designer jeans, the ones that tell the others on the street that he's an all-right dude. Sometimes it's for kicks, just to see the fear and loathing on the face of his victim. Sometimes it's to show the rest of us who's really on top. Ultimately, it's a game he will lose, but while he plays it, he can have the illusion at least of winning.

We're tired of asking why, of trying to understand. But if we think we have won something when a Bernie Goetz shoots four of these youths, we, too, live with illusions that will never be realized; we, too, are playing a game we're bound to lose.

The increasing separation between the black poor and the rest of society grows ever more dangerous. There are no walls high enough to contain the rage, no police force large enough to provide the protection we seek. That will come only when we find a way to reach across the gulf that now separates us so widely, when the cold statistics about being black in America take on human meaning, when we are prepared to deal with the powerful stereotypes that live inside us and that determine our attitudes and behavior, often against our conscious will.

As it is, when blacks come to mind at all, most of us don't see others like ourselves—the 53 percent of black families in America, for example, in which men and women struggle together to live decently, to love each other, to bring up their children wholesomely. In fact, when we think about the black family, most Americans generally don't see men at all. Only women—welfare mothers whose several children all have different fathers. Black women whose morals are so lax, whose lifestyle is so alien, they warrant contempt and anger, not ordinary human concern.

We don't see Shirley Cabey and Eula Canty—women who live without husbands through no fault of their own, who have managed to keep families together under tremendous odds, who weep helplessly because they can't protect their children in

neighborhoods where danger lurks on every corner. We don't
see Eddie Canty standing an agonizing vigil at his son's bedside,
wondering how this could have happened to him and his family.
We don't see the Ramseurs, a husband and wife in a long-term
marriage, who watch in impotent desperation as their son is
taken over by the culture of the streets in Claremont Village.

Most of us don't see either the 50 percent of young black men
who are unemployed, a figure that's more than four times higher
than it was just twenty years ago. Or the 70 percent of black
teenagers, ages fourteen to nineteen, who cannot find work of
any kind. Or the 25 percent of black men under the age of
twenty-five who have never held a job at all. Or the median
family income of blacks which, despite some economic gains for
a few, is $12,429, less than 56 percent of white income and
falling slowly but steadily since 1970, when it peaked at just
over 61 percent. Or the fact that murder is the most common
cause of death among black youths under the age of twenty-five
—1 in 21 murdered last year, a figure that represents 41 percent
of all the homicides in the country. Or the reality that among
blacks between the ages of twenty and twenty-four, there are
only 45 marriageable men for every 100 women. The rest are
either unemployed, dead or in jail. Nor do many notice the
infant mortality rate in the Bronx: 16.3 for every 1,000 live
births, compared to 10.6 in the United States as a whole.

These are cold statistics. But they tell a story of hopelessness.
Of a people who feel dispensable and disposable, who learn
early on that they don't count in the world. A story of im-
potence. Of boys who see men who have never had work, men
whose only surcease from the daily pain of emasculation comes
out of a bottle or a needle. A story of futility. Of women who
dream of traditional weddings and homes with picket fences they
know will never be theirs. A story of desperation. Of babies
dying because their pregnant mothers couldn't afford the prenatal
care that might have saved them. A story of rage. Of children
living without hope—children who know before they're half

grown that they're likely to die young and, worse yet, that their society will not mourn their loss.

We can call them lazy, say they're unwilling to work at the tough jobs, to work their way up as others of us did not so long ago. And undoubtedly there's some justice in the complaint at times. But the larger and more compelling reasons lie not in a given people's unwillingness or inability to pull themselves up by their bootstraps, but in the fact that, for most of them, the straps have been so shortened as to be almost nonexistent.

Since the Civil War, Americans have been able to count on a thriving economy to put their willing hands to work. The immigrants who came in such large numbers found jobs in the industrial sector of the work force. They were mostly menial jobs, it's true. But there was also the hope that next year, or the next, or the next, they'd do better. And if not them, then their children. Millions of children of immigrant families grew up with the parental words ringing in their ears: "I do dirty work, but you'll do clean work."

For American blacks, it has always been different. But even they could look toward tomorrow with hope. Troy Duster, a black sociologist, writes: "The layering of hopes and aspirations, of 'how it's going to be for the children,' is centuries-old. In slavery, the frontier of hope was abolition and freedom. At the end of the Civil War, the hope focused on Reconstruction. At the turn of the century, with lynchings and intimidation in the South . . . the hope riveted on the idea of migration North. With *Brown* v. *the Board of Education*, the hope shifted to the courts and legal redress. With the Civil Rights and Black Power movements, hope transformed to direct action."

That's changed now. The American economy is no longer so vital. The decline in manufacturing jobs, the increase in automation and in advanced technical occupations requiring higher skill levels, mean fewer jobs for the young and the less well educated of any color. The plant closings, so disproportionately high in the northeastern sector of the country, the movement of industries from cities to suburbs, from North to South, from the United States to foreign nations, affect us all. But for those who remain behind in the cities, the effect is most devastating. And that means black youths and their families in very large numbers.

For a variety of reasons—not least of them housing and job discrimination—blacks can't follow jobs to the suburbs. In New York City alone, the white population declined by 1.4 million in the decade between 1970 and 1980. Nationally in the twenty years between 1960 and 1980, the white population in the suburbs increased by 22 million. In the same period, the black suburban population grew by less than a half million.

More cold statistics, beneath which lie tragedy, heartbreak and human waste, as the plight of urban blacks becomes more and more desperate. As industry and the more affluent move away, the tax base of the city erodes, services become more problematic, schools decline into holding cells rather than the avenues of mobility they used to be. Students, when they come at all, sit listlessly, looking out at the world with dead eyes and dead hopes, their teachers' words falling numbly upon their inner certainty that no one cares and nothing counts.

"Harlem is no longer the promised land—it never was for today's manchild," writes Claude Brown. Entrapped in their own lives, these black youths have now trapped us—the "respectables," whether white or black—in ours. There are no excuses for them, at least none that make sense. But like it or not, they share the world with us, and we had better come to understand who they are, how they got to be this way, and what we, as a society, can do to instill once again the sense of hope and promise that must be theirs if we're to live in peace together. Otherwise we are consigned to an unending escalation of the present state of war between us.

AUTHOR'S NOTE

At 7:00 a.m. on Monday, January 7, 1985, I answered my phone to hear a familiar voice at the other end of the line saying, "I'm going to make you an offer you can't refuse." So began my connection with the case of Bernhard Goetz and the New York subway shootings.

My own instant response to the news of the event was, "Good! Someone finally gave it back to those damn kids"—sentiments I was ashamed of, even as I understood that I couldn't wish or legislate them away. While my immediate personal discomfort didn't leave me, it was eased by the fact that I heard similar feelings echoed all around me, whether in urban San Francisco, liberal and vanguard Berkeley, or rural Wisconsin and Ohio, where I happened to be lecturing during the days shortly after the shootings occurred. As the chorus grew more sustained and the ambivalence less in evidence, however, my personal uneasiness increased and was soon matched by a growing social concern.

Roger Straus, the editor who made that telephone call, knew that I was riveted by the case. He knew, too, that I believed from the start that this was not just another episode in New York City's daily ration of violence, that the incident had opened up levels of anger that most of us had only been dimly aware of before, that an event had taken place that would force us to look at ourselves in some new way.

Still, I thought he must be mad. I lived on the wrong side of the country, I reminded him. I had a psychotherapy practice that required a consistent presence in my office each week. Impossible, I said. But all the time I was protesting, I was also thinking how right he was: This might, indeed, be an offer I couldn't refuse.

I have lived in California for enough years to call it home. Yet I have never fully considered myself a Californian. No matter how much I have wandered, New York, the city of my childhood and early adult years, has remained an important part of who I am, how I think, and what interests me.

I grew up on the streets of the Bronx, just minutes away from what is now Claremont Village. From time to time over the years, I've gone back to the old neighborhood, to walk the streets of my childhood, to remember what it was like then. But I hadn't been there in some years, largely because each time I spoke of wanting to go, a New York friend would warn me off with stories about burned-out buildings and dangerous streets. If I agreed to take on this task, I knew I'd have no choice but to spend some time in the Bronx—walking those streets, meeting the people who live there now, talking to the families of the young men who were shot. The idea excited me.

Ten days and several phone calls later, I was on my way to New York. For the next several months, I commuted between the two coasts, leaving San Francisco on Wednesday afternoon, after my week's clinical schedule was finished, and returning home on Saturday night or Sunday. From time to time, I gave myself the luxury of a full ten-day stay. But those were rare.

I talked to hundreds of people about the case and have probably read every word that has been written. One New York newspaper reporter deserves special mention here. *Newsday's* Carole Agus's fine feature story on Bernie Goetz provided some background material available nowhere else. I interviewed some people formally, others more casually as I met them in my wanderings. I spoke with people who knew Bernie Goetz when he was a small child and those who have known him in his adult years. I met neighbors, classmates, teachers, friends of the family. But although I had many chances to observe him over the months, I never met Bernie himself because he refused all my requests for an interview.

Readers will undoubtedly notice that, except for public figures and the principals in the case, others remain nameless. The notoriety that surrounded the shootings and the intensity of feelings on all sides made most people uneasy about being identified. Therefore, it was necessary for me to promise anonymity and confidentiality before they would speak freely. But there's no reason for secrecy about the debt I owe to them. Without their generosity in sharing with me their time and their knowledge, this book would not have been possible.

My commute to New York is over now that I've written the story of Bernie Goetz in this time of madness. But my connection with the city, its people, and its problems will remain forever a part of me, as will my concern for a society whose inequities have too often made all of us both victim and victimizer.